W9-AXK-938

Writing Stories

Fantastic Fiction from Start to Finish

DAVID L. HARRISON

SCHOLASTIC
REFERENCE

To Sandy,
the best part of my story.
— DLH

Library of Congress Cataloging-in-Publication Data
Harrison, David Lee, 1937–
Writing stories: fantastic fiction from start to finish / by David L. Harrison
p. cm. — (Scholastic guides)
Includes index.
1. Fiction—Authorship—Juvenile literature. I. Title. II. Series.

PN3355.H335 2004
808.3—dc22   2003061297

0-439-51914-4 (POB)
0-439-51915-2 (PB)

Book design by Kay Petronio

10 9 8 7 6 5 4 3   05 06 07 08

Printed in the U.S.A.   23
First printing, July 2004

CONTENTS

CONTENTS

INTRODUCTION

Have you noticed how some people have a knack for writing stories? They don't seem to work at it; they're just naturally good. But writers work harder than people realize. Their secret is that the better they do their job, the easier it looks.

Taking a single thought and turning it into a great story—ah, that's the fun of being a writer. But a story doesn't just happen. No matter how good an idea is it won't grow into a satisfying story without some gentle coaxing by a hard-working writer.

Every story is different because every writer is different. Each of us tells our story like no one else can. But if you follow a few basic guidelines, you can turn your story into a winner.

If you want to become a writer—and I think you do—this book is for you. Someday, when people tell you you're just naturally good, smile. You don't have to tell them all your secrets.

Ready? Turn the page and let's get started.

CHAPTER ONE

Getting Started

The most important lesson in the first half of this chapter is learning how to tell a story. Together we'll turn a memory into a story by looking at all the elements that make up a story. After that we will write our memory as a story. This process can be called: think about it, talk about it, write about it.

In the second half of this chapter, I'll give you eleven tools and four techniques that writers use. Armed with these fifteen helpers, you will be ready to write a new story.

Here are five important terms you will find in this book:

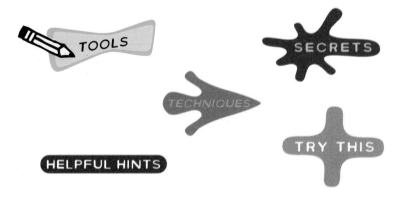

TOOLS

SECRETS

TECHNIQUES

TRY THIS

HELPFUL HINTS

 **TOOLS** are physical, tangible things. Carpenters use hammers and screwdrivers. Writers' tools include idea files and journals. We pick them up and use them when we need them.

 **TECHNIQUES** are keys that start the ignition of our imagination. Good writing techniques include giving ourselves choices, answering questions, playing the what-if game, and turning problems into stories.

HELPFUL HINTS are there to help you think. Sometimes a small clue is all we need to get started.

 **SECRETS** are important statements about writing. Once you understand the secrets of writing, you are well on your way to becoming a writer.

 **TRY THIS** gives you practice on the subject we've just been talking about.

BEGIN WITH AN IDEA

First comes the idea. Without that beginning thought, a character is just a character. A place is just a place. A problem, no matter how bad, is only a problem. Here is a quick way to find an idea that you can tell as a story:

Think of a funny experience you've had.

Got one? Good.

Now you have something to talk about. We begin by talking because talking is easier than writing. After all, hunters acting out the hunt and healers casting out evil spirits probably told the first stories. Telling a story teaches us a lot about writing one. Here's how.

Think About It

MY MEMORY

One night when I was six, I ate so many tacos that I still reeked of garlic the next morning at school. My teacher moved me to the front row so my breath wouldn't kill off any of my classmates.

Funny? Yes.

Story? No.

A story tells us more than **what** happened. We want to know **why**. And **when**. And **where**. And **how.** We want to know how things **look**. And **sound**. And **smell**. And **taste**. And **feel**. We want to **be there**.

What do you think a story is? I've read many definitions, but they all include three ingredients: character, conflict (problem), and resolution (solution). In this book I'll use *problem* to mean the same thing as conflict and *solution* to mean the same thing as resolution. We'll say that a story is what happens when we give a likable character a problem and watch to see how he or she manages to solve it.

TRY THIS

Practice Thinking About a Funny Memory

Describe your funny memory in a sentence or two. Below that write these questions and think about the answers:

- Why did it happen?
- When did it happen?
- Where did it happen?
- How did it happen?
- How did it look?

- How did it sound?
- How did it smell?
- How did it taste?
- How did it feel?

HELPFUL HINT

You don't have to answer every question. Telling a story calls for choosing the best details, not all of them. The list is to help you remember the details of the memory.

HELPFUL HINT

Something that happens in real life may not be a complete story. Our memory gets us started. After that our imagination may need to add a few "facts" along the way or leave some out. We're not writing for a newspaper, we're making up stories!

Talk About It

I love storytellers. They sing and sway, lure us into their tales, and make us their willing captives. Story writers only use words. That's why every word must be chosen with care, like sorting through gravel for diamonds.

But whether we are telling a story or writing one, we need to understand the elements of a story and what they do. In this chapter, we'll practice using those parts to *tell* a story. In Chapter Two, we'll put them to work when we *write* a story.

For now, imagine me standing in front of you. You are my audience. How can I get you to listen to me? You'll wander away and do something else if my first words don't grab you immediately. I'll start like this:

MY TACO STORY

Beginning

(We'll talk more about Beginnings in Chapter Two on page 40.)

> "If garlic could kill, I would have died in first grade. So would half my class. It started like this."

Think you can do better? Do it. Think of a championship, blue ribbon opening for your own memory story.

HELPFUL HINT

Try out several beginnings—four or five, at least. You'll like one better than the others.

Characters

(We'll talk more about Characters in Chapter Two on page 42.)

> When I was six, my mother and dad and I lived in a little town in Arizona called Ajo (Ah-ho). Mr. and Mrs. Geiger lived next door. She was motherly and liked to talk. I loved her cooking. He was funny and leathery and smelled of cigarettes. You never knew what he might say.

Now you've met my main characters. Who are yours? Introduce them to me. Make some notes so you don't leave anybody out.

Situation

(We'll talk more about Situation in Chapter Two on page 45.)

> One evening my parents were going out. Mrs. Geiger was cooking Mexican food and she invited me to eat with them. I begged until my folks said yes.

That's the situation that led to my experience. Think about the situation for *your* memory. What do I need to know to understand what is about to happen?

Problem

(We'll talk more about Problem in Chapter Two on page 50.)

Stories always have problems. Now that you've met my characters and know the situation, here's how my problem began:

> Mr. Geiger had invited company, too. The small house sounded like a parade was

marching through with grown-ups laughing and calling to one another in every room. Everywhere I walked, the air dripped with spicy smells from Mrs. Geiger's steamy kitchen. I didn't feel like talking and laughing. I wanted to eat!

At last, we sat down around a long table crowded with deep bowls and platters on hot pads. On a plate for me Mrs. Geiger built a mountain of beans and rice and a tortilla and an enchilada. On top of the peak she plopped a thick, brown taco bulging with ground beef, grated cheese, diced olives, sliced lettuce, and chopped tomatoes. Garlic, grease, and hot sauce soaked through the taco shell and flowed down the sides of the mountain like lava. The smell alone would make a meal.

I ate every bite.

Mr. Geiger noticed.

"Honey," he said to Mrs. Geiger, "David and I want another taco."

I felt like a balloon with too much air.

"No thank you," I said, holding up my hands. "I'm full."

Mr. Geiger winked and growled, "Nonsense! No one ever quits after just one of Mrs. Geiger's tacos!"

> The second taco plopped onto my plate.
>
> "Thank you," I said in a small voice.

Did your problem start off small and grow bigger? Can you see how mine did? One taco, small problem. Two tacos, much bigger problem!

Action

(We'll talk more about Action in Chapter Two on page 52.)

So what did I do about my problem?

> Mr. Geiger chewed fast and swallowed hard. I hoped my throat wasn't leaping up and down like a ball on a string the way his was.
>
> "David and I want another taco!" Mr. Geiger told his wife.
>
> "Nooo!" I said.
>
> PLOP! came the third taco onto my plate as heavy as a bowling ball.
>
> "Thank you," I said.
>
> Mr. Geiger winked and chewed. His bulging jaws crushed and ground his taco.
>
> I fixed my eyes on his jaws and matched him chew for chew. The last bite paused halfway down my throat like it was looking for a spot left in my stomach to land.

Part of the fun of telling a story is building excitement and suspense. Don't hold back. Wave your arms. Roll your eyes. Cry, laugh, sniff, shout. Shrug your shoulders. Hold your nose. Leap around.

Do you see places in my story that you could act out? When I tell it, I make sounds, pat my tummy, chew and swallow, move my Adam's apple up and down, speak with Mr. Geiger's grown-up voice and then with my little boy voice.

HELPFUL HINT

Make the funniest parts of your story funnier. The silliest parts sillier. The embarrassing parts more embarrassing. Storytellers are actors. You're onstage. Make me laugh!

HELPFUL HINT

If things didn't happen precisely the way you're telling them, that's okay. This is one time when telling a whopper isn't called fibbing. It's called storytelling! I don't remember exactly what Mr. Geiger said that night. He kept teasing me to eat more tacos. I made up the dialogue to make things more interesting.

Dialogue

(We'll talk more about Dialogue in Chapter Two on page 54.)

You can do a lot with dialogue. Letting your characters talk to one another beats trying to explain what they're thinking. It's faster and more fun. Even when you're the only one talking, dialogue breathes life into the story. For example, I could tell you about what happened next like this:

        Every time Mr. Geiger and I finished a
    taco, he called to his wife and told her that
    we both wanted another taco.

        I kept telling him no, but it didn't make
    any difference.

> More tacos kept landing on my plate.

Or like this:

> "David and I want another taco!" Mr.
> Geiger told his wife.
>
> "Nooo!" I begged.
>
> PLOP!
>
> "Thank you."

I repeat the same dialogue for the fourth, fifth, sixth, seventh, and eighth tacos that we stuffed down ourselves that night before we finally groaned to a stop.

> **Mr. Geiger always says,**
>
> *"David and I want another taco!"*
>
> **And I always reply,**
>
> *"Nooo!"*
>
> **Then comes:**
>
> *PLOP!*
>
> *"Thank you."*

Solution

(We'll talk more about Solution in Chapter Two on page 65.)

Every story needs a solution to the problem. My solution in the taco story was to keep choking down tacos until Mr. Geiger stopped. Thank goodness he did!

> After eight tacos, Mr. Geiger's great
> crusher jaws slowed to a stop like they had
> run out of oil. With a wheeze and a final
> wink, he eased back from his plate and
> gingerly touched his stomach.
>
> "David doesn't want any more tacos," he said.
>
> "Thank you," I whispered. There didn't
> seem to be room left in my body for a voice.
>
> Someone carried me to the sofa.

How did you solve your problem? Remember that it's okay to exaggerate if you need to. Do you think Mr. Geiger really said, "David doesn't want any more tacos?" Or that I really had to be carried to the sofa? So I was exaggerating a little. But it sure makes the solution funnier than if I'd simply said,

> After eight tacos, Mr. Geiger and I were
> too stuffed to eat another bite. He leaned
> back in his chair, and I tottered over to the
> sofa and collapsed in a heap.

The more you practice telling about your memory, the more it will begin to sound like a story.

Ending

(We'll talk more about Ending in Chapter Two on page 68.)

Learning how and when to end a story is so important that all of Chapter Three also talks about the subject. The ending is not the same thing as the solution, but it usually comes shortly after it.

The *solution* to my problem ended that night when Mr. Geiger finally quit eating. But the *end* of the story happened the following day when I showed up at school with killer garlic-breath.

> The next morning at school the girl beside me complained to the teacher.
>
> "Miss Merrill," she said, "somebody in here smells real bad!"
>
> It didn't take Miss Merrill long to sniff me out. I was exhaling deadly rays of garlic.
>
> I spent the rest of the day perched in the front row where only the chalkboard was in danger of cracking and peeling.
>
> I didn't mind. I'd done something that no one else had ever done.
>
> I'd matched Mr. Geiger taco for taco.

How did your experience turn out? If you need a better ending, make one up. I did.

The girl beside me complained about my breath to Miss Merrill. True.

Miss Merrill moved me to the front row to keep me from breathing on everyone. True.

I felt proud of keeping up with Mr. Geiger in our taco-eating contest. True.

But ...

I did *not* sit there gloating to myself about matching Mr. Geiger. I was probably embarrassed. But being embarrassed at the end of a story doesn't make a funny ending. Gloating does. So I gloated.

Write About It

It's easier to write when we know what we want to say.
Don't worry if the first draft of a written story seems less exciting than what you've been telling. It's hard to roll your eyes and wave your arms when you're writing! It's harder to make your reader "see" you rolling your eyes and waving your arms. But there are ways of getting that job done.

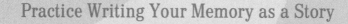

TRY THIS

Practice Writing Your Memory as a Story

1. Write fast. We'll talk about rewriting later.
2. See how many parts of the story you can identify:

   - Beginning
   - Characters
   - Situation
   - Problem

   - Action
   - Dialogue
   - Solution
   - Ending

3. Put the story away where you can find it later.

When you practiced your memory-based story, I said it was okay to stretch a few points to make the story better. Another way is to change your "memory" entirely. Start with some part of an experience that you like and make up a story to go with it. Let's play with someone else's memory to see how it works.

THE MOUSE AND THE ANTS MEMORY

In a writing workshop in Malaysia, I asked each student to choose a memory to think about, talk about, and write about. A boy who lived near the rain forest remembered when he was four years old and found a dead mouse covered with red ants on his bathroom floor.

Is that a story yet? No, it's only a memory. We still need a lot of how, why, when, and where information to turn his experience into a story. But which story? I see more than one. First, we have to decide what the problem in the story will be.

Problem One: The boy is afraid of ants.

Why do ants frighten him? I don't know. How about this?

- He lives near the jungle.
- Sometimes spiders get into the house, and lizards, and even snakes.
- But worst of all are the red ants, whose bites burn.
- Everyone hates and fears the red ants.
- Especially the boy.
- When he was very small, ants marched across the floor.
- The ants found him in his bed and bit him.
- He still has bad dreams about them.

A story based on such a memory might begin this way:

Story One

Early one morning a boy shuffles into the bathroom, yawning as he flips on the light. He's barefoot and wearing pajama bottoms with no top. His feet slap softly across the smooth tile.

What he sees on the floor makes his eyes widen.

A brown mouse lies there next to the toilet. The mouse does not run away. It remains still. It's covered with something. What?

The boy leans closer.

Red dots. Ants! The mouse is dead and it's covered with red ants! They're all over the floor! Crawling up between the boy's toes!

He feels the first hot stab as red ants swarm across his feet and start up his ankles.

Yelling in pain and fright, the boy stumbles backward from the room.

"Help!" he cries, plunging down the hall toward the kitchen. "Help me!"

What if we change the boy's problem? Instead of being afraid of ants, let's make the mouse his pet. See how that changes everything? Now we're not worried about ants. We feel sorry for the boy because his pet just died. The first idea is scary. The new one is sad.

Problem Two: The mouse is the boy's pet.

Same boy, same mouse, but different "facts" set the stage for a new problem.

- **The boy recently found a small mouse in the forest.**
- **The boy is always bringing home small creatures, but this one is his all-time favorite.**

☀ He loves her so much that he named her Georgette, in memory of his grandmother.

☀ Each morning he slips out of bed early to hold Georgette and stroke her soft fur.

Story Two

The boy wakes early and sits on the side of his bed. Stepping softly so he won't disturb his family, he moves to the box on the floor where Georgette lives.

"Georgette?" he whispers. Her box is empty. His brows wrinkle above his nut-brown eyes. "Georgette?"

"I'll find her," he assures himself. "Last time, she was in the bathroom."

On bare feet he enters the bathroom, shuts the door with care so it won't click, and turns on the light.

Georgette lies on the floor beside the toilet. He knows at once that she is dead. From across the room he sees the army of red ants marching over her small, helpless body.

"Georgette!"

His cry sounds like a wounded animal.

His family wakes right away. At once they know what's happened.

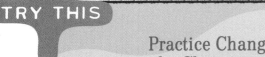

Practice Changing the Story by Changing the Problem

1. **Write this down:** When a boy was four, he found a dead mouse covered with red ants on his bathroom floor.

2. Make up at least one other problem that might lead to a different story.

You have just learned a very valuable secret about writing.

SECRET #1

Fiction writers may change what happened to make a better story.

We began this chapter with a memory-based story as a fast way to get started. Writers borrow from their memories all the time, and now you know how to do it, too.

But writers know plenty of other tricks. Here are eleven tools and four techniques to help you.

TOOL # 1

KEEPING TRACK OF YOUR IDEAS

An idea file is like a pantry stocked with food—but this pantry holds food for thought. We don't use everything we put there, but we want to keep plenty on hand.

Get a manila folder and mark it IDEAS. When you see something interesting, clip it out or make a note about it and slip it into your idea file. I have several folders of clippings and notes like this one from a newspaper:

Death Valley Claims Its Last Lonely Prospector. Seldom Seen Slim, eighty-six years old, earned his nickname with the way he lived—a recluse for fifty years in a desolate corner of Death Valley.

After all those lonely years, Slim was the last resident of Ballarat, now a ghost town. The last of Ballarat's seven saloons shut down in 1917, after the gold and silver mines petered out, but Slim stayed.

Slim always said, "I got no people . . . I was born in an orphanage. I don't get lonely . . . I'm half coyote and half wild burro."

Last Tuesday, Slim was found ailing in his run-down trailer in Ballarat's ruins . . . he lived only five days. A simple funeral is

planned Saturday in Boot Hill ... the first
burial in Ballarat in half a century.

Interesting articles make us think and wonder. Think like a writer along with me.

Seldom Seen Slim chose to live alone for fifty years in a ghost town in the desert. Don't you wonder about him?

What was Slim like? I wish I'd met him, sat beside him in the shade of his trailer, and listened to his stories. He must have had hundreds.

If you're thinking like a writer, ask yourself why he didn't go somewhere else. Why did he stay in Ballarat when, one by one, friends and neighbors left town?

I haven't written about that old prospector yet. Perhaps I never will. Does Seldom Seen Slim inspire you to make up a story about him? You may be the one who writes about him.

Good ideas take time to develop. Don't worry if you read something in your idea file and can't think of anything to write about it. Be patient. For years I kept an article about a little pig that ran away from the farm and found his way to a nearby town. I read that article many times, but nothing happened.

Then, one night, guess what? The pig suddenly turned into a story. I found my pen and started writing. That newspaper clipping from my idea file became a book called *Piggy Wiglet and the Great Adventure*.

TOOL # 2

KEEPING TRACK OF YOUR IDEAS— A WRITER'S JOURNAL

Who keeps journals? Most writers do. Some write in theirs nearly every day and others only write when something happens that they want to remember. Paula Graham interviewed several authors and wrote a book called *Speaking of Journals.* She asked how old they were when they started keeping journals. This is what they told her.

- Jean Craighead George started her first journal when she was ten.
- Jacqueline Woodson began keeping journals in fourth or fifth grade.
- Terry Tempest Williams was seven or eight.
- James Cross Giblin was ten.
- Jennifer Owings Dewey was eight.
- Naomi Shihab Nye was in second grade.
- I was twelve.

My first journal was a small notebook with lined paper. I used it mostly to write about insects that I caught for my collection. I also wrote about a bat I caught and a cave I crawled through. These days I like larger journals with unlined pages. I like to sketch without lines getting in the way.

What do you put in a journal? Just about anything. Your journal belongs to you. Some people not only write and sketch in their journals, they stuff all sorts of keepsakes such as pressed leaves or ticket stubs between the covers. Your journal is about you. Write down what you think, where you go, what you see and do.

What do you want to remember? A movie? What was it about? Did you like it or not? Why? Did you want to read about the subject or make up a story about it?

Have you tried your luck cooking? Have a favorite recipe? What happened the first time you tried it? Put it in your journal.

HELPFUL HINT

If this is your first journal, don't let all those blank pages scare you. A friend of mine had a hard time writing in her first journal. Those empty white pages looked so important that she was afraid to make the first mark. But once she finally started, there was no stopping her. Today she writes books.

How does a journal help? Have you forgotten a funny joke? Forgotten some of the things you did on a trip? When you write about something in your journal, you can go back and reread it later, even *years* later. That's the next best thing to being there again.

Today I do a better job of describing butterflies and bats and caves in my stories because, when I first saw them and they were fresh in my mind, I wrote about them in my journal.

TOOL # 3   LETTERS

I keep lots of them, especially ones that contain facts or tidbits that I might use. Letters also give writers good examples of how people think and express themselves.

TOOL # 4   SCRAPBOOKS

Scrapbooks hold a lot more than pictures and old birthday cards. They store a treasure of memories that help me write.

TOOL # 5   BOOKS

You don't have to own a lot of books to be a writer. That's why writers love libraries! Thousands of books line library shelves, waiting for us to check them out and learn something interesting to write about.

TOOL # 6   STORAGE

Writers are pack rats. We never know when something might be useful. I store things I want to keep in boxes, drawers, and cabinets.

TOOL # 7   MAGAZINES

*National Geographic*s fill one corner of our garage. The living room piles up with magazines and newspapers. I clip articles, poems, stories, and odd facts that catch my eye. The clippings usually make it into one of the idea folders.

TOOL # 8 MANUSCRIPTS

I keep copies of every draft of everything I write. Sometimes I find a thought or expression in an earlier version that I'm glad I didn't throw away.

TOOL # 9 DICTIONARY

Writers are finicky about words. A careless choice throws the reader off track and creates confusion. When in doubt about the proper meaning or spelling of a word, look it up.

TOOL # 10 THESAURUS

Most people overuse favorite words and phrases. Like, you know what I mean? Writers look for fresh, imaginative ways to tell their stories. A thesaurus lists alternative words to say what needs saying.

TOOL # 11 RHYMING DICTIONARY

Most people don't even know there is such a thing as a rhyming dictionary. If you're writing poetry, it's one of the best books you can have because it gives you every sound that rhymes with the sound you're thinking of. But here's something that even fewer people know: prose gets better, too, when you choose similar sounds and rhythms to help tell your story.

Launching Into a Story

Now here are four techniques that help start writers' imaginations:

TECHNIQUE # 1 ▶ **GIVE YOURSELF CHOICES**

It is tempting to take the first idea we find and get busy writing. I've done that many times. But starting a story before I've given myself enough choices to think about may not produce my best work. I've learned to slow down and ask myself what is so special about this idea. Can I think of other ideas? Maybe better ways to tell it?

How giving yourself choices works. Think about the boy and the mouse. The first problem was that he hated ants. So why not write his story that way? We could have done that. Then again, what if the mouse was the boy's pet? We were giving ourselves choices.

Having choices helps us discover the best story. In *The Book of Giant Stories*, which has three stories in it, I wanted the same boy to meet a different giant in each story. That part would always stay the same. Everything else could change. The boy could meet the giants anywhere. They could meet for different reasons and do different things. I soon thought of three ideas that I liked.

But then I thought of another idea. Now I had four ideas for three stories. While deciding which three I liked best, I thought of a fifth choice. A sixth and a seventh. I couldn't stop. Thinking up giant story ideas became a game. I kept going until I had a list of thirty-eight. That's what I call giving yourself choices!

When I finally chose three ideas to write, I had a wonderful time. After all, the three I chose were the cream of the crop.

TRY THIS

Practice Giving Yourself Choices

1. Read this list of story possibilities:
   - The swing breaks at school and somebody falls.
   - A blind boy goes fishing alone.
   - Our teacher gives us the wrong test.
   - My sister is acting strangely.
   - The neighbors' dog barks in the middle of the night.
2. Pick one of these ideas to think about.
3. Write the idea in your journal.
4. Make a list of choices about how you could tell a story using that idea.
5. Keep the list and add more choices as you think of them.

Giving ourselves choices helps us think, and thinking helps us write. Now you can see why this is such a valuable secret.

SECRET #2

Writers give themselves choices.

Here's another technique to kick-start your imagination:

TECHNIQUE # 2   **ANSWER THE QUESTION**

I know you're good at asking questions. One time I asked students during a school visit for a list of questions. Two weeks later they mailed me 1,500! It took two years to write a book of answers. Most of those answers could have been turned into stories. Here are five examples of the questions:

1. What sort of child was Albert Einstein?
2. Do insects freeze in the winter?
3. What was the first musical instrument?
4. How do you tame a lion?
5. Who invented gum?

Pick a question and answer it. Let's choose number three to play with. What can we do with this question: What was the first musical instrument?

Hmm. Music is an old idea. Way back when people lived in tribes and clans they must have danced and sung around their campfires. Their first musical instrument would have been simple.

Answer Number One

One night three guys in animal hides slouch half asleep on logs around the fire in front of their cave. A burning limb shifts and shoots sparks onto one of the men. Grunting in pain, he leaps to his feet, slaps his scorched skin, and runs around the fire yelling.

His companions poke each other and grunt at how funny he looks dancing around the fire slapping himself and yelling. Making fun of him, they jump up slapping themselves and dance after him, yelling and carrying on like kids on their first woolly mammoth hunt.

The first musical instrument was the human body.

Answer Number Two

Unless…

Other clan members wander out to see what the ruckus is about. An old man, too tottery to dance, creaks himself down to enjoy the show. Soon he's clapping his hands and swaying to the rhythm. Croaking and yipping, he pats the ground to keep time with the dancing.

Aha! The first musical instrument was the ground!

Answer Number Three

Unless…

A spear fisherman limping along the beach picks up an old conch shell with a hole worn through the top. This guy has had one of those days you don't want to think about. He broke his best spear on a turtle and he's hungry enough to eat sand.

He grabs the shell and shakes it. A shriveled-up little tidbit rattles around in there. Trying to get it out, he huffs across the hole.

No luck. Naturally.

What comes out instead is a loud, clear note.

The hunter jerks the shell away from his mouth. He looks around to see if he's alone. He grins. That sound is so cool! Forgetting his empty stomach, he carries the shell back to camp, blowing on it as he goes.

Other clan members hurry from the cave to hear this amazing new sound.

The guy becomes famous. He retires from spear fishing and starts playing at weddings and bar and bat mitzvahs.

Well, okay, that last part is silly.

But it's okay for writing to be fun.

Anyway, the first musical instrument was a conch shell.

TRY THIS

Practice Answering a Question

1. Start a new list in your journal called THE FIRST MUSICAL INSTRUMENT.
2. Put down what we have so far:
   - Body
   - Ground
   - Conch shell
3. Make a list of other things that early musicians could blow, beat, pound, rub, shake, rattle, or roll.
4. Pick one and imagine a story about who invented that instrument and how.

See how quickly you can build a list of story ideas? And you got them all by making up answers to a single question. The next time someone asks you a good question, jot it down in your journal, along with one or two quick thoughts about story possibilities.

PLAY THE WHAT-IF GAME

Sometimes writers stir their imaginations
by asking themselves what-if questions
and then attempting to answer them.

This is one of the best techniques and one of the easiest to use. Sometimes kids turn it into a game. "What if I woke up one morning and I could fly?" "What if a watermelon seed grew in my tummy?" "What if I could talk to animals?"

TRY THIS

Practice Turning What-If Questions Into Stories

Make a list of what-if questions in your journal. Here are some suggestions to help you get started:

- What if a girl finds out that her best friend is planning to run away?
- What if a boy sees someone shoplifting?
- What if a girl who can't swim sees a friend drowning?
- What if a boy suddenly starts understanding animals' thoughts?

Puzzle over these what-if questions and write down some of the answers that you think of.

Notice that you have started with a list of situations that can quickly turn into problems. And, as you think of how these problems might be solved, you are discovering some interesting characters. You are on your way to writing a new story.

SECRET #3

Answering questions can create stories.

On Page 9 I described a story as what happens when we give a likable character a problem and watch to see how he or she manages to solve it.

TECHNIQUE # 4

TURN PROBLEMS INTO STORIES

Sometimes we get ideas for stories by thinking about problems that someone has to solve. Think about some of your favorite books. Many of those stories are about boys or girls who feel lonely, frightened, lost, or confused. In other words, they have problems to overcome.

Think about the people you know. Do any of them have problems? We all have a few. Some are as unimportant as a wrinkled shirt. Others are serious enough to make a good story.

Practice Turning a Problem Into a Story

Start a list in your journal called WORRIES AND PROBLEMS.

Here are a few suggestions to help you get started:

- A boy has trouble waking up on time.
- A girl has problems at home.
- A boy doesn't "get" math.
- A girl has bad dreams.
- A boy wishes he could be popular.

The character in your story doesn't have to be you. And the story doesn't have to be about you. But if your list gives you a story idea, then you've just learned another secret.

SECRET #4

Writers turn worries and problems into stories.

CHAPTER TWO

Elements of a Story

In Chapter One, we talked about how to turn memories into stories, and we identified nine elements of a story. In this chapter, we'll look carefully at those elements to make sure you understand each one. Dialogue is included although it's more related to the way we write than it is to the other elements of a story, and some stories have no dialogue at all. But in most stories, dialogue plays such a crucial role that I decided to put it on this list. Here is what we'll talk about:

* Idea
* Beginning
* Character
* Situation
* Problem
* Action
* Dialogue
* Solution
* Ending

In *The Wizard of Oz,* Dorothy and her friends follow the Yellow Brick Road to the Emerald City to find the Wizard. They think that he is all-powerful and that only he can grant their wishes.

It turns out that the Wizard is just a regular person—like you or me—standing behind a curtain. He yells into a loudspeaker, fills the room with smoke and lights, and pretends he's a wizard. But in the end, because of him (or in spite of him), Dorothy and her friends find what they're searching for.

Writers are like the Wizard of Oz. We stand behind the curtain of our words, inventing characters and giving them problems to solve. Then we set them off down the road in search of solutions. How do we do it?

FIRST COMES THE IDEA

We can start by thinking of a problem that somebody needs to solve, or a character who seems interesting. It helps to think about both at the same time.

Examples based on real stories:

1. Wooden puppet, sometimes naughty, wants to become a real boy. (Pinocchio)

2. Pig born runt of the litter fears for his life. (Wilbur in *Charlotte's Web*)

3. Hero from another planet disguises himself as a mild-mannered reporter. (Superman)

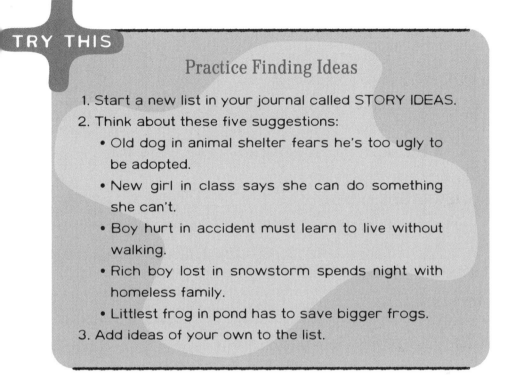

TRY THIS

Practice Finding Ideas

1. Start a new list in your journal called STORY IDEAS.
2. Think about these five suggestions:
   - Old dog in animal shelter fears he's too ugly to be adopted.
   - New girl in class says she can do something she can't.
   - Boy hurt in accident must learn to live without walking.
   - Rich boy lost in snowstorm spends night with homeless family.
   - Littlest frog in pond has to save bigger frogs.
3. Add ideas of your own to the list.

Do you see a story lurking in these situations? I'm going to choose one that I like. It's the second one, the new girl in class who says she can do something she can't.

I'll make up a story about that girl, and you make up your own as we go along. If you like another idea better, then use that one. Follow what I do, and then use the same techniques with your idea.

What do we know about this main character so far?

1. She is a girl.

2. She is new in class.

3. She says she can do something that she can't.

We'll come back to the new girl on page 47.

Now we have to:

- Think of a *beginning* that grabs the reader's attention.
- Develop her into a real *character*.
- Establish the *situation* for her story.
- Decide how she got into this *problem*.
- Watch the *action* as she attempts to solve her problem.
- Find out what her *solution* is.
- Figure out the best *ending*.

BEGINNING

Maybe you've heard the expression: You only get one chance to make a good first impression. Writers will tell you that the same idea applies to stories. We may get only one chance to catch the reader by the shirt and yank him or her right inside our story.

Have you ever started to read a book and decided it was just too boring? That happens to everyone. Sadly, not all stories are great ones. In this book, our job is to figure out how to get our stories off to good beginnings. We don't want readers yawning and putting our stories down before they read, and *love*, every word!

In the beginning, strangely enough, writers don't always worry too much about the beginning. The trick is to get started. But we know that sooner or later we'll need an opening so amazing that readers forget to snap their gum. When that time comes, it's important to know what we're looking for. For example, we need to recognize a good first sentence when we see one. Here are four examples of what I mean:

> "Where's Papa going with that ax?" said
> Fern to her mother as they were setting the

table for breakfast. (*Charlotte's Web* by E. B. White)

"I am on my mountain in a tree home that people have passed without ever knowing that I am here." (*My Side of the Mountain* by Jean Craighead George)

The Mole had been working very hard all the morning, spring-cleaning his little home. (*The Wind in the Willows* by Kenneth Grahame)

"It was the hottest part of summer, and the sun on my back was digging in its claws like a scared tomcat as I trudged down the dusty road, heading north." (*Bristle Face* by Zachary Ball)

TRY THIS

Practice Looking for Strong First Sentences

1. Write in your journal: GOOD FIRST SENTENCES.
2. Read the first sentences of at least twelve books.
3. Write your favorite choices in your journal.
4. Record the name of each book and who wrote it.
5. Keep the list and add to it when you find more good examples.

The first sentence is not the whole beginning. You need to read more than one sentence to get the feel for how a story begins. But the point is that the very first sentence is *really important*. It's the beginning of the beginning. We need to make it good! Shortly after the first sentence—or maybe even in it—we'll meet our main character, get an idea about the situation, and find out what kind of problem our character has to try to solve.

CHARACTER

Developing a character is a big job. What would Harry Potter books be without Harry? If the Grinch didn't steal Christmas, who would? Take away Winnie-the-Pooh, and who would Christopher Robin play with? Without characters, there is no adventure. The story cannot go on.

The characters in our favorite stories may be as magical as Harry, ornery as the Grinch, or lovable as Pooh Bear. Heroes or villains, strong or weak, magical or regular everyday sorts, they are the stars of the show. The leading character can be just about anything. In *The Giving Tree*, Shel Silverstein's main character is a tree!

Developing a character that readers will like and root for takes a little practice. On page 25 I described a valuable writers' tool: the journal. The next two exercises show you how useful your journal can be.

FAVORITE CHARACTERS

TRY THIS

Learn From Characters You Already Know

1. Write in your journal FAVORITE CHARACTERS.
2. Think about characters you remember from books, magazines, television shows, movies, and plays.
3. Write their names down the left-hand side of the page.
4. Beside each name jot down two or three traits that describe that character.

There are three kinds of characters: *main* characters, the stars; *supporting* characters, the ones who help make the stories happen; and *minor* characters, who add necessary details to the background of the story.

Here are five examples of supporting characters.

1. In *Clifford the Big Red Dog*, Clifford needs Emily Elizabeth, Cleo, and T-Bone.

2. In *Sarah, Plain and Tall*, Anna needs Papa, Caleb, and (of course!) Sarah.

3. In *Julie of the Wolves*, Miyax needs Daniel and the wolves—Amaroq, Silver, Nails, and the others.

4. In the *Harry Potter* books, Harry needs the Dursleys at home and the whole cast of characters at Hogwarts.

5. In *Shiloh*, Marty needs the dog Shiloh, his family, and Shiloh's cruel owner, Judd Travers.

Minor characters can be almost anyone or anything. Like these:

* Ants that mess up a picnic
* An angry voice in a crowd
* An unidentified thief in the night

Writers see interesting characters everywhere. Observe the people and animals you see or read about.

Remember Seldom Seen Slim (from my idea files)? Look for characters like Slim in newspaper and magazine stories.

I read a story about a woman who kept an eight-hundred-pound hog in her house for protection against intruders. Now *that's* a character!

Maybe you know someone who has a habit that you can borrow for one of your characters. A friend of mine used to save the rolls that toilet paper comes on! She kept them in sacks under her bed. She said she really didn't know why she did that. Toilet paper rolls just looked useful to her. Her nutty habit might be useful in a story, too.

FACES IN THE CROWD

TRY THIS

Practice Looking for Characters

1. Start a new list in your journal called FACES IN THE CROWD.

2. Describe interesting faces in your journal. Like this:

    • Man with gold earrings in both ears, wearing baseball cap turned backward. Lopsided grin. Laughing and talking with friends.

    • Girl covered in freckles. Blond hair parted in the middle. Pretty blue eyes.

    • Woman with thick glasses. Walking her black lab on a leash. Holding a book close to her round face. Bright red scarf. Gray hair. Scuffed shoes.

3. Add to your list from characters you see in movies and on television.

HELPFUL HINT

Take your journal with you when you might see plenty of people. Shopping centers are excellent places to people-gaze. So are sports events, parks, amusement centers, and restaurants.

Your notes will grow the more you people-watch. Every face is interesting when you take time to look and observe. One novelist saw a woman in an airport and made up a whole novel about what she thought the woman's story might be.

SITUATION

Writers may argue about which is the most important element of a story.

Some say it is character.

"Without strong characters, you can't have a strong story," they will tell you.

Others believe it is situation.

What do we mean by situation? It is the time of the story. The place. It is the setting. It's how we arrange our characters so that they will meet at the right moment and in the right circumstances. Situation explains why the characters have the problems they do and why they attempt to solve them the way they do. Situation creates a world big enough and complete enough to hold our characters and their story.

Some writers call this the setting. Others call it situation. In this book, we'll call it situation. Here is an example of how changing part of the situation changes what the reader expects to happen.

Let's say that we're writing a story about Josh, a boy who recently lost his father. Josh has to take a job at night after school to help support his mother and sister. Josh feels lonely. He misses his friends. He's always tired, and his grades are falling.

How should we let the reader know that Josh is a sad boy? A cemetery can be a sad place, especially to someone who has recently lost a father. But what happens if we get carried away describing the cemetery? Such things can happen in the first draft.

> Rain-swollen clouds turned the night dark as a coffin. Near the iron gate, spidery willow limbs draped over the cemetery wall and wove themselves into a black curtain big enough to hide a crouching man. Josh approached the tree, wrapped in his own thoughts. But the rustling leaves seemed unnaturally loud, like something was stirring among them. What was that? Josh stopped dead still. Did something just move behind those limbs?

This situation isn't about Josh, is it? It's about the cemetery. Not only that, our reader now expects something to happen that isn't going to happen. Anton Chekhov was a great Russian writer who believed that if the opening of a story mentions a shotgun hanging over the mantel, then that shotgun must be fired before the story ends. What he meant was, don't set up false clues. Don't make your reader think something you mention is important if it isn't. If this story isn't going to involve the cemetery, we should write the paragraph more like this:

> Heavy clouds made the night as dark as Josh's mood. A weeping willow just inside the cemetery draped its slender limbs over the wall to touch the ground beside the walk. Leaves rustled like they were whispering

```
secrets. Josh walked past without looking up.
He had too many other things to worry about.
```

Now the reader knows that the cemetery isn't important to the story. Josh walks by it, thinking his own thoughts, so we follow him to find out where he's going and what's on his mind.

Does this situation fit the story better? I'd say yes. But is it the best way to let the reader know about Josh, the boy who has lost his father? Probably not. Know what I'd do? I'd whack the whole paragraph, cemetery and all, and look for a better way to explain Josh's situation. I'd put him in school, daydreaming. Or at work, tired and trying to stay awake. Or in his room, holding his father's picture. I'd look for a faster way to take the reader straight into the story of Josh and his problems.

Back to our story about the new girl...

Let's give our character a name. I'll call her Kara. Give her a different name if you wish, but in my story she's Kara, eleven years old. All we know about Kara so far is her name and age and that she's told a lie in school.

Imagination time! Kara doesn't exist until we bring her to life and make her exist. She is whoever we say she is. Her history is whatever we say it is. She is *our* character. We need to imagine her and then explain her to our readers.

But making up things willy-nilly about our character doesn't help much. We need to know when Kara's story will take place. And where. And why. What are the circumstances that make this story happen? We need to know the situation.

SECRET #5

Character and situation are connected.
Change one and the other changes, too.

Our story proves how tightly character and situation are related. Look at these three ways to set the stage for Kara's story. Each time we change the situation, something also happens to Kara. Her character changes because of the new situation. And, every time, her problem changes, too.

One: The story takes place in the present.

- Kara's parents are divorced.
- Kara has been living with her father on a ranch in Texas.
- She has just moved to a big Eastern city to live with her mother.
- Her new classmates tease her about her Texas drawl.
- They make jokes about Texas.
- They ask if she knows any Indians.
- They want to know if she can rope cattle.
- Kara hopes they are all having fun together.
- She laughs and says, "Sure I can rope! Every girl in Texas can twirl a rope! Can't you?"

Problem for this situation:

- Her teacher, trying to be helpful, says,

    "That's wonderful, Kara! I know the class would love for you to show us how to twirl! Bring your rope in on Monday!"

- Kara is suddenly in big trouble.
- She has never twirled a rope in her life.

Two: The story takes place in the present.

- Kara has been living with her mother in a big Eastern city.
- She has just moved to a ranch in Texas to live with her father.
- Her new school has four rooms.
- The playground is dirt.
- The only sport is softball.
- Kara is bored and shows it.
- Everyone in class feels insulted by her attitude.
- Kara took two ballet lessons just before she moved.
- Trying to impress the other girls, she offers to teach them ballet.

Problem for this situation:

- Kara assumes that no one in such a little rural school will know anything about ballet.
- Too late, she discovers that one of the other girls is a trained and talented ballerina.

Three: The story takes place 100 years ago.

- Kara grows up living with her father on a ranch in Texas.
- Her mother died when she was born.
- Her father has remarried.
- Kara and her stepmother don't get along.
- Her father has sent her to live with her aunt in a big Eastern city.

- Kara missed a lot of school on the ranch.
- She can barely read.
- Boys in her new class tease her about the way she dresses.
- They tease her about the way she talks.

Problem for this situation:

- One boy tells her that she can't read.
- Kara blushes with embarrassment.
- "I can too read!" she blurts out.
- "Prove it!" sneers the boy, shoving a book at Kara.
- "Read something!"

Amazing, isn't it? Change a few details about Kara or the situation and the story takes off in a different direction.

PROBLEM

Stories are about characters and how they solve their problems. If we make the problem too easy, the reader gets bored. If we make it too hard, the reader doesn't believe the solution.

Example

Mr. Jones lives in town. He's out of ice. No big deal. He drives to the store, buys ice, and drives back home.

Too easy.

Yawn.

No story.

Mr. Brown, on the other hand, lives in the desert one hundred miles from the nearest town. He's out of ice, too, and he has no car. He'd have to walk one hundred miles to town, buy ice, and walk one hundred miles home.

Too hard.

No story.

Wait! What if Mr. Brown trains his dog to go to town! His faithful dog runs like the wind with a cooler strapped to his back, gets the ice, and races back home.

What do you think?

Get real!

No way.

No story.

The problem, like Little Bear's porridge, must be just right.

SECRET #6

The story seems more interesting when the problem seems important.

Back to our story about Kara...

Now we have three Kara-problems. We've given ourselves choices. In the beginning of a story we introduce the characters and the situation. But what does the reader want to know as soon as possible? The problem!

Which of Kara's dilemmas do you like best? Which one do you want to see her struggle to solve? Does she say she can twirl a rope, dance, or read? Do you have a different story in mind? I like the rope problem, so I'll go with it. Kids tease her about being a cowgirl from Texas until she blunders into claiming that she can twirl a rope.

Now what?

Well, now Kara must do something. She got herself into this mess. Only she can get herself out. How she does it is most of the rest of the story. Bring on the action!

ACTION

What is the plot? The plot is the way you decide to tell your story. What will your characters do? How will they attempt to solve their problems? How will everything work out? Plot deals with action. In this book, we use action to mean plot.

Writers agree that the plot is not the same thing as the story itself. The story is the idea. It is *about* something. Plot is the *how*. It is the structure of the story that helps us get where we want to go.

Stories have three parts: beginning, middle, and end. In the beginning, we introduce characters, situation, and problem. In the middle, our characters struggle to overcome the problem. At the end, the problem gets solved.

The middle part of the story is nearly always the longest, and it's where most of the action takes place. Our hero has a lot of problem-solving to do!

Solving the problem on the first try is too easy. A problem solved that fast can't be much of a problem. We want our own problems to be easy to solve, but we love it when the characters in our stories have to sweat it out until the very end. Just when our hero seems sure to win, something goes wrong and the situation looks more awful than ever. That's the stuff that wears out flashlight batteries when we can't stop reading after bedtime!

SECRET #7

Characters never solve their problem on the first try.

SECRET #8

Most of the story is action that leads to solving the problem.

We can change the action without changing the story. Here's what I mean:

Example

Fantastic Mr. Fox is about a clever fox who outsmarts three farmers who are out to kill him. That's the story.

The *action* is *how* it all happens.

How the farmers try to get Mr. Fox is part of the action.

How Mr. Fox outsmarts the farmers is part of the action.

This is what I mean. The farmers could try to kill Mr. Fox with poison instead of guns, and Mr. Fox could outsmart them by faking his own funeral. The story would still be about a clever fox outsmarting three farmers out to kill him.

Example

Little Boy's Secret, one of my books, is about a boy, captured by giants, who outsmarts the giants and gets away.

That's the story.

The boy's secret is that he is coming down with chicken pox, but I could have given him some other secret that would frighten giants without changing the idea of the story. I chose chicken pox because it seemed like a fun surprise, not because the story had to be told just that way.

Characters in longer stories often face more than one problem. That makes the action more complicated. The character no sooner gets past one problem than another one takes its place.

Example

Shiloh by Phyllis Reynolds Naylor

A boy named Marty meets a dog that follows him home. Its owner, Judd Travers, has abused the poor animal. As you might expect, Marty wants to keep the dog, but he is soon tangled up in several problems.

- **For the first time he finds himself keeping secrets from his parents.**
- **He invents ways to keep his sister away from the hidden dog.**
- **To protect Shiloh, Marty hurts a friend's feelings.**
- **He tells a half-truth to the dog's owner.**
- **Marty goes to work for the man he hates, Judd Travers.**

Saving Shiloh turns out to be much harder and far more complicated than Marty ever dreamed it could be.

DIALOGUE

We've talked about idea, beginning, character, situation, problem, and action. It's time to decide how you want to tell your story.

Your writer's voice. Everyone has a personal way of talking. You recognize the voices of people you know, and they recognize yours.

When you write, how you think and speak come through in the words you choose and how you arrange them into sentences. That's your writer's voice. It's your style. No one else on Earth has a writer's voice exactly like yours.

I told you at the beginning of this chapter that I included dialogue even though it is more related to how we write than to the other elements of the story. When you use dialogue, your writer's voice is still there, but sometimes your story works better when you share the stage with your characters.

Here are four ways to help keep your story moving along.

You Tell the Story

Sometimes writers tell (narrate) their story as if they are standing back, watching the action and describing it.

One nice thing about narrating is that you can explain to your reader what is going on, sometimes even before your character has figured it out.

Example

> Fox was about to get the surprise of his life. Every hen in the henhouse had learned kickboxing. Cackling softly among themselves, they peeked out through a crack and watched the unsuspecting thief slinking up the path toward his doom.

One of Your Characters Tells the Story

When your character speaks, your reader learns something right away about that character.

> "I smell chickens!" Fox told himself. "Straight ahead! A henhouse is full of juicy, plump chickens! Here I come, my delicious, darling, juicy, plump chickens!"

Your Character Talks but You Help

Even if your character is telling the story, you're busy adding important details to keep things moving along.

> "I smell chickens!" Fox told himself. "Straight ahead!" He had not eaten in three days. Not a fat mouse. Or a skinny lizard. Or even a sorry little grasshopper. He licked his lips and almost purred.
>
> "A henhouse is full of juicy, plump chickens!"
>
> Fox's tattered tail twitched. His hairy ears cocked forward.
>
> "Here I come, my delicious, darling, juicy, plump chickens!"

More Than One Character Talks

In some stories more than one character has something to say.

> "I smell chickens!" Fox told himself. "Straight ahead!" He had not eaten in three

days. Not a fat mouse. Or a skinny lizard. Or even a sorry little grasshopper. He licked his lips and almost purred.

"A henhouse is full of juicy, plump chickens!"

The henhouse leader pressed one eye against a crack in the wall.

"He's coming!" Lily whispered.

Unaware that he was being watched, Fox crept up the path.

"Ready, girls?" Lily whispered.

"Let him come!" came two dozen fierce voices.

"Where is he now?" someone asked.

"Shhh," Lily whispered. "Just outside the door."

Fox crouched, ready to spring.

"Here I come, my delicious, darling, juicy, plump chickens."

On the other side stood a determined flock of warrior hens.

Someone was in for the surprise of his life!

Learning to Write Dialogue

Characters need to sound natural. How does a writer learn to write good dialogue? Two words: Listen. Practice. Listen to conversations around you. Everyone talks differently. How do your classmates speak to one another? How do the members of your family communicate? Dialogue is not just about how high or deep our voices are, how loud or soft. Each of us has a rhythm to the way we speak.

- Some of us speak like we're in a hurry.
- Some of us go slowly and choose words with care.
- Some of us use worn-out expressions.
- Some of us change subjects in the middle of a sentence.
- Some of us interrupt others before they finish speaking.

We overhear bits of conversation all the time in restaurants and parks and stores and at school.

- "So I told her it was none of her…"
- "I freaked out man like I was like so totally like you know I thought I'd like totally like lose it!"
- "He won't understand. He never under-…"
- "I can't even think about that now!"
- "He's so cuuuute!!!"

TRY THIS

Practice Writing Dialogue

Write some short conversations in your journal for these combinations of characters:

- an elephant and a mouse
- a hero and a villain
- a teacher and a student
- a parent and a child
- a sister and a brother

Anthropomorphism

When animals or other nonhuman characters in a story start talking and behaving like humans, someone made up a long, tongue-twisting term for that: *anthropomorphism* (an-throw-po-**mor**-fism).

Cartoons on television are filled with anthropomorphic characters—that is, talking animals. *Charlotte's Web* and plenty of other books are filled with such characters, too. The fox sneaking up on the henhouse full of kickboxing chickens is another case of anthropomorphic animals.

Personification

When we crawl inside a nonhuman character and speak as though we were that character, there is also a term for that: *personification*.

Some fifth graders were studying world history and their assignment was to write personification poems about what they learned. Here's an example.

THE LEANING TOWER OF PISA
by Ryan Miller

I am the Leaning Tower of Pisa.

Come sit and lean with me.

I am in Italy.

I feel like I am going to fall.

I keep standing up.

I shelter people from the rain.

I know if I fall I may cause lots of damage.

I sense that I might fall.

```
I dream that I'll be visited.

I am 185 feet tall.

Come imagine leaning with me.
```

Now you have several ways to write your stories. Even though your own writer's voice will shine through in all of them, look for opportunities to mix up the methods to keep your stories interesting and moving along quickly.

You are learning more and more secrets that writers use to make their readers want to find out what happens next!

Let's take a break and talk about titles. The only story I ever wrote that began with the title was Detective Bob and the Great Ape Escape. I thought of the title late one night when I couldn't sleep. Some time after that, I wrote a story to go with the title.

Most writers agree that titles aren't easy. The title's job is to make us want to read the story. It should give us a clue, tease us a little, make us want to find out more. That's why some writers don't worry about their final title until the story is finished, or at least well along. As for me, I may change the title two or three times before I get it right. I usually start with a "working title" so that I can call the story something until its real name finally comes along.

TRY THIS

Practice Thinking of Titles

1. Read several book titles.
2. Pick out three favorites.
3. Why do you like them?
4. Make a list of three choices for Kara's story.

Back to our story about Kara...

We're about ready to start writing Kara's story, so let's give ourselves a "working title." We can change it later if we think of something better, but for now we ought to pick something that makes the reader curious about the story.

Here are my three suggestions. You don't have to use any of them for your own story, but since I don't know yours, we'll use mine for now.

1. The Longest Weekend

2. Lasso Trouble

3. The Cowgirl Who Couldn't Twirl a Rope

I like the last one best. It's more personal because we know there's a certain kind of person in the story. It tells us what kind of activity to expect. And it gives us a strong clue about the problem.

Now you are ready to write. I've outlined your story with some helpful hints to keep you thinking about Kara and her woes. You don't have to explain everything on this list. And you can certainly add ideas of your own. I wish I could see how your story turns out, because everyone will tell it differently.

THE COWGIRL WHO COULDN'T TWIRL A ROPE
by You

Beginning

Think about your beginning this way:

- Concentrate on introducing the character, setting the stage, and presenting the problem.
- As your story unfolds, reread your beginning to see if you still like it.
- When you finish the story, polish that beginning until we need sunglasses to look at it.

Character

Introduce us to your main character as soon as you can. Tell us about her, but not all at once.

- She's lived in the Texas sun all her life.
- How did she get here to a school in a big city? (You choose the city.)
- How does she feel surrounded by city kids who tease her about being from Texas? Don't tell us, show us.

HELPFUL HINT

We want to like Kara even though she's made a mistake. Being new in school isn't always easy. We hope she manages to solve her problem in a way that teaches her a lesson but at the same time earns her the respect of her new classmates.

Situation

Where are we now? Give us the picture.

- Is Kara in her classroom?
- What does it look like?
- Is she in the cafeteria?
- Is she on the playground?
- Is she standing outside of the school?

Tell us what we're seeing.

- What does the school look like?
- Is it different from her school back home?

Tell us about this teasing business.

- Does everyone give Kara a hard time, or just a few students?
- Tell us who these kids are and what they look like.
- How do they sound to Kara?
- Does their speech sound as strange to her as her Texas drawl does to them?

☀ Is Kara's teacher nice?

☀ Is there anything we need to know about him or her?

Problem

Tell us about the day when Kara's real troubles begin.

☀ Do her classmates tease her (again!) about being from Texas?

☀ Do they call her a cowgirl?

☀ Do they ask her if she can rope cattle?

Help us feel like we're right there with Kara.

☀ Does the teasing make her feel bad? How do we know? Show us.

☀ Does she hope the other kids are laughing with her and not at her?

☀ Does she try to tease back?

This is a big moment. We want to feel how she feels and watch what she does. When someone laughs and says, "Can cowgirls twirl a rope?":

☀ What does Kara say?

☀ How does she say it?

☀ Does she try to laugh with everyone else?

The trap is set. Tell us what happens next.

☀ What do the other kids say when Kara claims that she can twirl a rope?

☀ Does someone else tell the teacher what Kara is saying?

☀ What does Kara's teacher say?

☀ Does she invite Kara to show the class how to rope?

☀ When?

☀ What does Kara say to the teacher?

☀ What does she say to herself?

Action

Kara has told her classmates that she can twirl a rope like a cowboy even though she has never tried. She was only kidding, but the joke went wrong and now her teacher and all the kids in her class are expecting her to bring a rope to school on Monday to show them how to twirl a rope.

What will Kara do? This is going to be the rest of the story. Remember that the reader wants to see her try and fail a time or two before she finds the solution. Think like a writer. Here are some possibilities.

1: Kara's first plan is to teach herself how to twirl a rope over the weekend.

Can you imagine her trying to dream up a way to learn rope twirling? Make it worse by assuming that she is afraid to explain her problem to her mother.

- She looks up roping in an old book. No help.
- She tries twirling the cord from her bathrobe. Knocks over a lamp.
- She calls a hardware store looking for real rope. Again, no help.
- Kara gives up this solution.

2: In a panic, Kara tries to find a real cowboy to come in to show her classmates some rope tricks.

In a big city? No way. But she's running out of time. It's now Saturday night and she still doesn't have a solution to her problem!

- Kara reads the newspaper to see if there's a rodeo in town. Nope.
- She looks in the yellow pages under cowboy. No such heading.

* She decides against calling her father in Texas. All that would do is get her into more trouble.
* Besides, *she's* the one who is supposed to do the twirling.
* Kara gives up this solution, too.

3: Can you think of other ways that Kara tries to solve her problem?
Add to the list if you can.

This may seem like a cruel place to leave poor Kara dangling, but we need to take a quick time-out.

SOLUTION

A moment comes in most stories when the character sees what it's going to take to solve the problem. After all the confusion, anger, frustration, fear, failure, and maybe even danger, the character knows what has to be done. What comes next may be more dangerous than anything before, but it's the only way. At all costs, no matter what happens, this is the solution. We follow word by word as the determined character accepts the truth.

Kara has tried everything she can think of to get out of her mess. Nothing has worked. She's at the end of her rope (groan). Now she sees the solution. And because she understands that it's the only way, she must do it.

Your story may turn out different from mine, but here is how I might finish Kara's story.

Solution

Kara knows that on Monday she must tell the truth.

Her teacher and classmates may never forgive her for lying to them. But she has to live with herself, and the only way she can do that is to tell the truth and apologize.

Making the right decision, Kara feels calmer. Feeling calmer, she begins to think more clearly. Maybe she can't twirl a rope, but she can do plenty of other interesting things on a big ranch in Texas.

She starts making a list of things she *can* do:

- Milk a cow
- Throw a breakfast together for twelve hungry cowboys
- Saddle, ride, and take care of a horse
- Play a fiddle
- Line dance and two-step
- Chase off a rattlesnake
- Mimic an owl
- Help corral cattle

As Kara's list grows, her courage returns. On Monday she will be ready. Picture in your mind what happens on Monday, and then help us see it, too. Maybe Monday goes something like this:

> Kara comes to class without a rope. She looks calmer than she expected. Everyone asks why she doesn't have her rope with her. Her teacher looks puzzled, too, and asks if everything is all right. Kara manages to smile and assure everyone that she will explain.

Kara walks slowly to the front of the room, turns, and faces the class. What she does next takes all the courage she can manage. In a small but steady voice, she admits the truth, that she doesn't own a rope and has never tried to lasso anything.

The classroom is so quiet that Kara thinks she can hear her own heart thumping. Somehow she manages to stand straight and look back at all those staring faces. Everyone, including her teacher, waits for her to continue.

Kara's voice grows stronger. She apologizes for not telling the truth. She explains that all she wanted to do was make new friends and become part of the class. She says that on the ranch she saw a lot of cowboys rope cattle, but no one ever thought a girl needed to know such things.

Then she pulls out the list from her skirt pocket, unfolds the paper, and begins to talk about her life on the ranch. One by one, her classmates lean forward in their seats to listen. It isn't long before they start raising their hands and asking her questions. From the corner of her eye, Kara sees her teacher's face. She's smiling.

ENDING

It's time to end our story of the new girl in class who told her classmates she could do something she couldn't.

The ending comes right after the solution, but it's not always the same thing. It's the part that helps us remember the story and the character after we finish reading. It's the part that leaves us saying, "That was a good story!"

Endings are often short, maybe only a sentence or so. How should Kara's story end?

- Does Kara impress everyone with her honesty and courage?
- Do her classmates accept her?
- Does she feel better about herself?
- Does her story end with her standing in front of the class, smiling at her new friends?
- Does a popular girl in class invite her to spend the night?

We'll talk about endings in the next chapter and how they are related to beginnings. After you finish reading Chapter Three, come back to the beginning and ending of Kara's story and see what else you might want to do with them.

Remember how Kara's story started? She was Number Two in a list of five characters with problems. She's come a long way since then, and so have you. We made up her story together, but yours will be different from mine because we all have different storytelling styles. We don't sound alike or think alike or write alike. And that's what makes writing so much fun.

CHAPTER THREE

Ending Your Story

In Chapter Two, we talked about getting off to a good beginning. The most important thing about this chapter is learning how to end your story.

 I'll show you how the ending is tied to the beginning.

 We will talk about nine different ways to end a story.

 For each kind of ending, you'll get an example of how to start a new story.

How do you know when your story is finished? When the problem is solved. Sure, but there is more to it than that. The ending is not just the place where you stop writing. It is an important part of the story — just like the beginning is. You have to plan for it. Often you'll find that something in the beginning will show up again at the end.

TRY THIS

Practice Spotting Connections Between Beginnings and Endings

1. Pick three favorite stories.
2. Read the first page of each.
3. Skip to the end and read the last page.
4. Make a new section in your journal and mark it BEGINNINGS AND ENDINGS.
5. Write down what you notice about the connection between the way stories begin and end.

The genre of story you write (see page 85) may help you decide the best way to end it. Sometimes you start with an ending that helps you choose the beginning. There are many kinds of endings.

NINE WAYS TO END A STORY

ONE: Characters Change

If a character has changed since the story began, the ending may point out the difference.

Example

The Best Christmas Pageant Ever by Barbara Robinson

The six Herdman kids are the worst bunch in the history of the world. They lie and steal and smoke cigars. Teachers don't want them in their classes. Parents don't want their kids close to them.

At tryouts for the Christmas pageant, the Herdmans show up and take all of the good parts.

Everyone expects the Herdmans to ruin the play.

But the play changes the Herdmans.

When those roughnecks hear the Christmas story for the first time, they take its lesson personally. As the Angel of the Lord, skinny-legged Gladys shouts out her lines. She thinks her words are extremely important and everyone needs to hear them.

The pageant turns out to be the best ever. The story ends like this:

```
When we came out of the church that night
it was cold and clear, with crunchy snow
underfoot and bright, bright stars overhead.
And I thought about the Angel of the Lord—
Gladys, with her skinny legs and her dirty
sneakers sticking out from under her robe,
yelling at all of us, everywhere:

"Hey! Unto you a child is born!"
```

The story is over, but the Herdmans' unexpected change makes us stop to think and wonder. The ending seems to last after the covers of the book are closed.

TRY THIS

Practice Endings Where the Character Changes

1. Start a new journal page called CHARACTERS THAT CHANGE.
2. Make up some beginnings and endings where the character changes. Here's an example:

Beginning: A boy with no friends becomes a bully.

Ending: The boy changes and helps someone.

TWO: Characters Don't Change

Sometimes what makes a story good is that the characters *don't* change. In spite of everything, they go right on being just the same as always.

Example

The Giving Tree by Shel Silverstein

A tree loves a little boy. Giving him her apples and shade makes her happy. When the boy becomes a man, the tree gives him her branches. When he is older, she gives him her whole trunk. The man grows old and tired. The tree has only a stump left to give, but it's enough.

```
    "Come, Boy, sit down," the tree tells the
old man.

    "Sit down and rest."

    And the boy did.

    And the tree was happy.
```

The tree and the boy have grown old, but nothing else has

changed. She still loves him and gives him all she can. He still accepts her gifts. The ending makes us like the tree even more.

TRY THIS

Practice Endings Where the Characters Don't Change

1. Start a new journal page called CHARACTERS THAT DON'T CHANGE.
2. Make up some beginnings and endings where the character does not change. Here's an example:

Beginning: A girl's puppy jumps on her for joy as the girl leaves for school.

Ending: When the girl comes home after a bad day, her puppy still jumps on her for joy.

THREE: Surprise

When we read a mystery, we often don't find out "who did it" until the end. Getting surprised is part of the fun.

Example

The Little Boy's Secret by David L. Harrison

A boy leaves school early with a secret to tell his mother. On his way home he meets a giant who demands to know the secret. The boy is soon surrounded by three giants. Reluctantly, he gives in and whispers his secret in their ears. The giants yell and run away. The boy finally makes it home and tells his mother his secret. She feeds him and puts him to bed.

> The next morning when the little boy woke up, he was covered from head to toe with bright red spots.
>
> "Now I can tell everybody what my secret was," he said with a smile. "My secret was . . . I'm getting the chicken pox!"

When I started that story, I needed something to scare away giants. I decided to give my boy character the chicken pox. Of course his mother would love him and take care of him. My secret was safe until the final two words in the story. I planned the ending as part of the story, down to the last two words in the last sentence.

TRY THIS

Practice Endings That Surprise

1. Start a new journal page called SURPRISE.
2. Make up some beginnings that can end with a surprise. Here's an example:

Beginning: Tim fills the bird feeder each evening, but every morning it is completely empty. Something or someone is stealing all the birdseed during the night.

Ending: Tim finally gets up in the middle of the night and shines a flashlight on the feeder. The thief, a young raccoon, is helping himself to a free meal.

FOUR: Warning

Some stories are scary. Some are scary and funny at the same time. A favorite way to end such stories is with a warning that the bad guys may be back. Moviemakers love this sort of ending. They might want to make a sequel. Is the story over, or is it just over for now? The ending adds to the scariness.

Example

The Wish Giver by Bill Brittain

Thaddeus Blinn, a spooky little fat man with strange, glowing eyes, shows up at the church social and says he can grant people's wishes for fifty cents. Three kids learn the hard way that their wishes come true in awful ways that leave them miserable. Here comes the warning at the end:

> As far as I know, Thaddeus Blinn is still out there, roaming the highways and byways of this land of ours. So if you're ever at a carnival or a fair or a community social and you meet a little fat man in a white suit, with a thick watch chain across his red vest . . . have a care!
>
> Look closely at his eyes.
>
> Especially if he tells you he can give you anything you ask for.
>
> Before you take him up on his offer, think it over. Think very carefully.
>
> Maybe there's something else you'd rather spend fifty cents on.

The ending makes us think that the story may go right on somewhere else. As long as Thaddeus Blinn is still out there—somewhere—other people are having problems. We must be careful. We don't want to be next!

Practice Endings with a Warning

1. Start a new journal page called WARNING.
2. Make up some beginnings that could end with a warning. Here's an example:

Beginning: A strange dog with one ear bigger than the other appears in the village, looks up at the sky, and howls. He howls all day. That night, a boy in the village disappears. The dog is never seen again.

Ending: If a strange dog with one ear bigger than the other appears in your town, looks up at the sky, and howls, beware. Someone could disappear. It could be you!

FIVE: Joke

Usually, bad guys don't win. We love to laugh at their expense and see them get what they deserve. One good way to do that is to play a joke on them.

Example

Fantastic Mr. Fox by Roald Dahl

Boggis, Bunce, and Bean are three rich, nasty-tempered farmers who vow to kill Mr. Fox for stealing from them. They dedicate their lives (and the entire book) to getting the fantastic fellow. Mr. Fox tunnels into their cellars and steals all he wants, but the three villains think they have trapped him in his hole.

At the end they are sitting in the rain, waiting to shoot him when he finally comes out.

> "He won't stay down there much longer now," Boggis said.
>
> "The brute must be famished," Bunce said.
>
> "That's right," Bean said. "He'll be making a dash for it any moment. Keep your guns handy."
>
> They sat there by the hole, waiting for the fox to come out.
>
> And so far as I know, they are still waiting.

Everyone loves to laugh at the bad guys when someone plays a good prank on them. It's even funnier when they don't know that the joke is on them.

Practice Endings with a Joke

1. Start a new journal page called JOKE.
2. Make up some beginnings that could end with a joke.
Here's an example:

Beginning: A mean man who can't see well pulls his poor little dog around by a rope around its neck.

Ending: The little dog switches places with his friend, a much bigger dog, who pulls the man around by the rope. The frightened bully can't believe how much his little dog has changed. He apologizes and promises never to be so mean again.

SIX: Hope

We readers like stories that fill us with hope and make us feel as if something good could happen.

Example

Stuart Little by E. B. White

Stuart is born into a human family but he's a mouse. He's a brave little mouse and gets along with everyone except the family cat, but he misses having someone his size to be with.

When the family rescues a small bird named Margalo, Stuart thinks she is beautiful. Stuart and Margalo become friends, and Stuart is heartbroken when Margalo leaves one day to return to the wild. He climbs into his tiny car and sets out to find his friend. He hasn't found her when the book ends, but he has high hopes.

> Stuart . . . climbed into his car and started
> up the road that led toward the north. The
> sun was just coming up over the hills on his
> right. As he peered ahead into the great land
> that stretched before him, the way seemed
> long. But the sky was bright, and he somehow
> felt he was headed in the right direction.

Because Stuart believes that he will find his friend, we hope so, too. The ending makes us feel that the story goes on. Stuart will search the land until someday, somewhere, he and Margalo will be together again.

TRY THIS

Practice Endings That Inspire Hope

1. Start a new journal page called HOPE.
2. Make up some beginnings and endings that provide a feeling of hope. Here's an example:

Beginning: A girl and her mother become homeless. They have little to eat, and no place to wash their clothes.

Ending: A caring teacher helps the mother find a job. At last the girl can see a brighter future.

SEVEN: Reassurance

Some stories are about trust and reassurance. They remind us that parents love their children and take care of them no matter what. Such stories leave us feeling warm and comfortable.

Example

Little House on the Prairie by Laura Ingalls Wilder

When Ma and Pa and Mary and Laura leave their little log cabin in Wisconsin, they travel by covered wagon all the way to Kansas, where the family settles into life on the great prairie. There they encounter wolves, fire, storms, Indians, a panther, and illness.

When Pa hears that the government is going to make them move because they have settled in Indian Territory, the family packs up and leaves their house on the prairie. On the move once again, they travel across the plains by day and sleep at night in their covered wagon. As always, the girls put their trust in Pa and Ma. Pa sings them to sleep at night and reassures them that everything will be okay.

> Softly and slurringly [Pa's fiddle] began a long, swinging rhythm that seemed to rock Laura gently.
>
> She felt her eyelids closing. She began to drift over endless waves of prairie grasses, and Pa's voice went with her, singing.
>
> "Row away, row o'er the waters so blue,
>
> Like a feather we sail in our gum-tree canoe.
>
> Row the boat lightly, love, over the sea;
>
> Daily and nightly I'll wander with thee."

These children are homeless, too. But they have their mother and father and one another. The children know that their parents love them and will always keep them safe. No matter what happens, Laura feels reassured that Pa and Ma will take care of them.

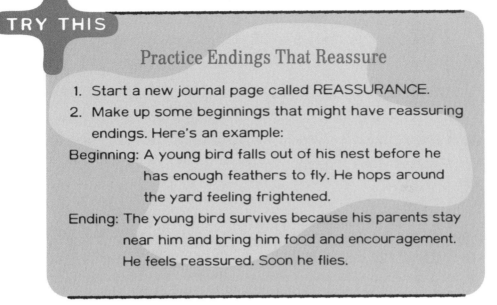

TRY THIS

Practice Endings That Reassure

1. Start a new journal page called REASSURANCE.
2. Make up some beginnings that might have reassuring endings. Here's an example:

Beginning: A young bird falls out of his nest before he has enough feathers to fly. He hops around the yard feeling frightened.

Ending: The young bird survives because his parents stay near him and bring him food and encouragement. He feels reassured. Soon he flies.

EIGHT: Ending at the Beginning

Some stories end where they started. The characters may go somewhere else and have an adventure, but sooner or later they come back to where they began.

Example

The Cows Are Going to Paris by David Kirby and Allen Woodman

The story begins with a field of bored cows and these words:

```
The cows have grown tired of the fields.
The cows are going to Paris.
```

After a number of adventures in the city, the cows return to their pastures. The characters have changed. They've learned something from their adventure, and now they are happy to be back home. The story ends:

> Having been to the city, the cows see that
> there is something wonderful about visiting a
> new place. But they know that there is
> something just as fine about coming home.

The story is finished. We get the idea that the cows aren't likely to leave again. They've had their fling. The cows' tale has come full circle, ending where it began.

TRY THIS

Practice Endings That Return to the Beginning

1. Start a new journal page called ENDING AT THE BEGINNING.
2. Make up some beginnings and endings that start and finish in the same place. Here's an example:

Beginning: Every morning a boy complains when it's time to wake up. He decides to run away from home so he can sleep all he wants to. He has no food. His clothes get dirty. He runs out of money. Finally he decides to come back home.

Ending: Next morning the boy wakes up and starts to complain, but he changes his mind. Home is pretty nice after all.

NINE: Coping with Problems That Can't Be Solved

Some stories present characters with problems they can't do anything about. Because they can't make their problems go away, they must learn to cope with them and somehow keep going.

Example

Good-bye My Wishing Star by Vicki Grove

Twelve-year-old Jens Tucker lives with her mother, father, and brother on a farm. Times are tough for farmers. One by one, families lose their property and move away.

The day comes when Jens's family must move, too. Leaving everything she has ever known—friends, school, the land—is the hardest thing that Jens has ever had to do. When her life seems ruined forever, an old man named Mr. Shire gives her this advice: "You can always keep home in your heart," he tells her, "wherever you may go." The story ends like this:

> I'm taking Mr. Shire's advice and carrying this place with me, hidden so deep inside that nothing can pull it out of my heart. I'll build on it. Everything I live from now on will sprout from it, like clover from seed.
>
> There have been so many things to say good-bye to. And now, something inside me is about ready for some hellos.

We want to cry for Jens, her story has been so sad. In the end, her family loses everything. Nothing can save them. Sometimes that's the way it is in real life. But the ending is an important part of the story. Instead of leaving us with the feeling that Jens's life is ruined forever, we watch her make peace with herself and with the family's terrible problems. The ending helps us believe that Jens has what it takes to survive her grief.

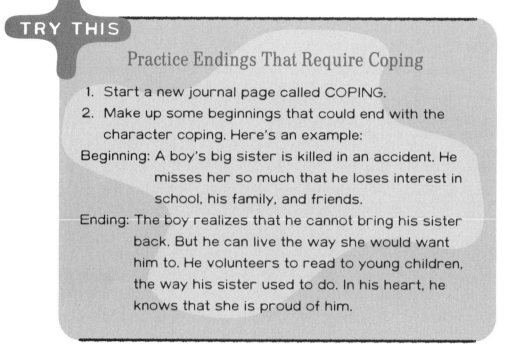

Practice Endings That Require Coping

1. Start a new journal page called COPING.
2. Make up some beginnings that could end with the character coping. Here's an example:

Beginning: A boy's big sister is killed in an accident. He misses her so much that he loses interest in school, his family, and friends.

Ending: The boy realizes that he cannot bring his sister back. But he can live the way she would want him to. He volunteers to read to young children, the way his sister used to do. In his heart, he knows that she is proud of him.

Turn back to the first page of this chapter and reread the beginning. I began by asking the question "How do you know when your story is finished?" I answered the question for you then. Now you can answer the question yourself. You know that the ending is part of the beginning. It is a vital part of the whole story. A story without a good ending is not a story at all — it may just be a report of something that happened.

CHAPTER FOUR

The Special Needs of Genres

In this chapter you will discover three important things about writing fiction:

✺ Good stories are more alike than they are different.

✺ Different kinds (genres) of stories have special needs.

✺ Genres sometimes overlap.

We will look at the special qualities of five major genres and the guidelines for each one. You can practice starting stories in all five of these fiction genres:

✺ Realistic

✺ Fantasy

✺ Science Fiction

✺ Historical

✺ Mystery

We use the word genre (**jhon**-ra) to distinguish one kind of fiction story from another. Realistic, fantasy, science fiction, horror, mystery, humor, historical, romance, and Western stories belong to different genres. But good stories are more alike than different, so it is not unusual for genres to overlap with one another. In this chapter I'll tell you about five kinds of fiction: realistic, fantasy, science, historical, and mystery.

REALISTIC

When we write about things we know, we write about real life in the real world. We make up a story based on something that happened or could happen.

Realistic stories are about real people facing real problems. Who they are, how much we like them, and how bravely and cleverly they deal with their problems make us want to read their stories.

When we make up a story about Kara, who gets herself into trouble by lying to her classmates, we are writing realistic fiction.

- Kara may not be a real girl, but she seems real.
- The situation makes her problem seem real.
- Under the right circumstances, that could happen to us.
- In the end, Kara shows courage and does the right thing.
- She behaves well, and we respect her along with her classmates.

Four Rules for Realistic Stories

1. The character seems real.
2. The situation helps us understand how the story could happen.
3. The problem is believable.
4. The character solves the problem.

If all four elements are present in your story, you are writing realistic fiction.

Example

In *Julie of the Wolves*, the young Eskimo girl Miyax is alone and without food in the great frozen tundra. There is no hope of finding enough food to stay alive. She is sure to starve to death. The only way she can think of to save herself is to make friends with a pack of wolves and share their food!

Does the character seem real? Yes. Miyax tells us about herself and how she got into the mess she's in. She seems quite real, and brave, and resourceful.

Does the situation help us understand how such an adventure could take place? Yes. We learn right away that Miyax is lost somewhere "in the crackling cold of the Arctic winter." We learn that no one can save her but herself. Her life depends on making friends with wolves. By her actions we learn that Miyax is resourceful and wise in the ways of her Eskimo heritage.

Is her problem believable? Yes—under these special circumstances. We'll never be in that situation, but Miyax is, and unless she can persuade those wolves to share their food with her, we can believe that she will die.

Her idea seems desperate and dangerous, which makes us want to read on to see if she succeeds.

Does she solve her problem? Yes. And she does it, to our amazement, exactly how she said she would.

So is this realistic fiction? Yes.

TRY THIS

Practice Starting a Realistic Story

1. Start a page in your journal called REALISTIC STORIES.
2. Make up a character who seems real.
3. Describe a realistic situation.
4. Think of a believable problem for your character.

FANTASY

Realistic fiction stories are supposed to make sense. Fantasy stories are make-believe. And their job is to make us believe, too. To see the difference between realistic fiction and fantasy, let's look again at our four rules of realistic fiction:

1. The character seems real.
2. The situation helps us understand how the story could happen.
3. The problem is believable.
4. The character solves the problem.

What happens if we break one of the rules? Well, we really can't change Rule Four. One way or another, the problem must get resolved. That leaves three choices: Character, Situation, and Problem. **But we also have to be careful about breaking Rule Three.** Unless we understand the problem and can believe that somehow our character can manage to solve it, or learn how to deal with it, we don't have much of a story.

That leaves Rules One and Two: Character and Situation. These are the rules to change when writing fantasy. Fantasy stories are filled with wonderful characters that exist only in the special situations we invent for them. They could never exist in the real world.

In fantasy stories we meet wizards, talking cards, flying nannies, a mouse raised as a boy, a girl who travels by clicking her shoes, fairy godmothers, and princes turned into frogs. We know there are no giants. Witches don't whiz around on broomsticks. Pigs don't carry on conversations with spiders (or anyone else). For that matter, spiders can't spell out words in their webs or capture hobbits and hang them head-down from trees.

But here is another of those big secrets.

SECRET #9

Not everything about fantasy is fantasy.

Example

In *The Book of Giant Stories*, my giants are big and my witches fly. Just the way they ought to be. Right? I could never allow my giants to fly or make my witches big. That simply wouldn't do! These are storybook fantasy characters, but they still have to live by the rules.

And who makes the rules? We do. After reading plenty of stories about giants and witches, readers have become experts. We get to say what will work and what will not work in stories about such characters. They can have some magical qualities, but otherwise they must behave themselves.

Example

In *Charlotte's Web*, Charlotte is a gifted spider if there ever was one. Wilbur and Charlotte meet in his pigpen. They think and talk like "normal" animals. We know about Wilbur's problem. We just hope that Charlotte can save him! The stage is set for magic.

When Charlotte does save Wilbur, we love her for her fantastic deeds. But she also has everyday spider kinds of worries. She still has flies to catch. She thinks about getting older. She thinks about her children who will come after her. We understand Charlotte and we like her because of her "real life" problems.

Example

Then there's Harry Potter, who lives a real but wretched life in a real house on a real street. No magic. Just misery. He's picked on by his cousin, Dudley Dursley, and scolded and punished constantly by Aunt Petunia and Uncle Vernon.

When magic visitors appear in the night, Harry's life changes forever. Before long he's off to a secret school that normal people could never find. But even at wizard school Harry still thinks and behaves like a real boy most of the time. He worries about making friends and doing well in school. He makes mistakes. He even has to put up with bullies.

Fantasy characters seem real enough at times, but they all have magical qualities that can only exist in their special situations. So what are the differences between realistic fiction and fantasy stories?

Four Rules for Fantasy Stories

1. Characters have **magical qualities that cannot exist in the real world.**

2. The situation **makes the fantasy seem possible**.

3. The problem is believable.

4. The character solves the problem.

Practice Starting a Fantasy Story

1. Start a page in your journal called FANTASY.
2. Make up a character who has at least one magical quality.
3. Describe a situation that makes the fantasy seem possible.
4. Give your character a problem that seems believable.

SCIENCE FICTION

Fantasy stories ask us to believe in wizards and trolls and talking animals. Science fiction stories start with what we know about the real world and ask us to believe in new possibilities. Before there were submarines, computers, and space travel, they existed in science fiction stories. Science fiction looks out from where we are now and imagines what might happen — in the past, present, or future.

No matter how strange some science fiction stories seem, there is the possibility that they *could happen*. Fantasy stories *could never happen* except, of course, in our imagination.

How do we switch gears from making up a fantasy story to making up a science fiction story? We know we can't change Rules Three and Four:

3. The problem still has to seem believable.

4. The character still has to solve the problem.

What does that leave?

If we want to change from fantasy to science fiction, change Rules One and Two. Most science fiction characters possess no magical qualities the way fantasy characters do. Their machines or weapons or houses or knowledge or the way they travel may almost seem magical, but that may be because they are more advanced than we are. Their science may be more developed than ours is. Or maybe they live in a time and place where we can't go, or at least we haven't been there yet.

How do we convince the reader to go along with adventures that sometimes seem so hard to believe? By inventing situations that make such adventures seem possible.

That is not always easy. For example, if we want to set our science fiction story in space, we may have a problem because most of us don't know enough about space to sound very convincing. We need to do research before we write about stars and gravity, planets and galaxies and comets, asteroids and black holes and unknown objects whizzing around in the cold darkness. More reading! But here's something else that will help.

SECRET #10

If you can't go to space, bring space to you.

Jane Yolen's book *The Robot and Rebecca and the Missing Owser* is jammed with characters from other planets. Everyone comes and goes and gets along together (well, almost everyone). We meet snakemen from the planet Hisssssss; owsers (three-legged doglike critters) from the K-9 galaxy; colorful children from the Rainbow galaxy; a thief from Chameleon III who keeps changing his shape; and all sorts of pets—from dragons and woolly muffles to weedsels and slate-colored marbeliters.

To help us believe that something like this could really happen, Jane places her story in the future. And who is to say what could happen by then!

Four Rules for Science Fiction Stories

1. The character **may be different from anyone we know, but seems possible**.
2. The situation **helps us understand how the story might really happen, someday or somewhere**.
3. The problem is believable **under the circumstances**.
4. The character solves the problem.

TRY THIS

Practice Starting a Science Fiction Story

1. Start a page in your journal called SCIENCE FICTION.
2. Describe a character who is different from us but who might possibly exist.
3. Describe a setting that makes the character seem possible.
4. Think of a believable problem for your character.

HISTORICAL

Remember that stories often include parts of more than one genre. Historical fiction is a good example. Historical fiction takes place in the past, but it might be a mystery, a romance, or just about any other kind of story, too.

Some historical fiction writers work hard to make their stories as true to life in those times and places as they can. Their stories spring from people and events of the past and are based as much as possible on real characters and places. Other authors make up stories that only sound like real places, people, and events. Either way, we have to learn about the times and places we want to write about.

Establishing a historical situation makes historical fiction seem real. I once had a story idea about a boy who lived in England nearly one thousand years ago. This make-believe character would be the son of a poor man who made charcoal to support his family. In my imagination, the boy would save the life of a prince. The grateful prince would reward the boy with an important job in the castle. As a result of his bravery, the boy would be able to help his family.

But I had a problem. I knew nothing about life in England one thousand years ago. What did people wear? What did they eat? How much was charcoal worth? How was charcoal made? What sort of house did a poor family live in? What did castles look like?

See how historical fiction works? I couldn't write my story until I learned more about my situation. Even though my story was going to be fiction, it wouldn't work if I didn't know my nonfiction facts.

You don't need to go farther than your library to prepare

for your historical fiction story. Before Scott O'Dell could write *Sing Down the Moon*, about a Navajo Indian girl, he had a lot of reading to do.

O'Dell's story takes place from 1863 to 1865, a time in our history when the United States and the Navajo are fighting with each other. Finally, soldiers are sent out to capture all Navajo and march them hundreds of miles to Fort Sumter in New Mexico. It is a terrible time for the Indians. Many die. Only a few escape to live in hiding, hoping to be left alone in peace.

The Indian girl and other characters in Scott's story are fiction. But the dates and times and places are real. The situation makes the story seem real, too. The characters' problem really happened. This is historical fiction. The author makes up a story that teaches us about a two-year period in our history and what it was like then to be a Navajo Indian.

Stories like this don't always have happy endings. Sometimes the characters can't solve their problems. All they can do is try to cope with them the best way they can.

Four Rules for Historical Stories

1. The character seems real **or is real**.
2. The situation **makes us feel like we're back in time**.
3. The problem is believable **and may have really happened**.
4. The character solves the problem **or learns to cope with it**.

See how realistic and historical fiction overlap? If someone one hundred years ago wrote a realistic story, today it would be considered historical fiction.

TRY THIS

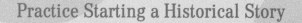

Practice Starting a Historical Story

1. Start a page in your journal called HISTORICAL STORIES.
2. Describe a historical character you'd like to write about.
3. Imagine the situation at the time your character lived.
4. Present your character with a believable problem to solve.

You don't have to write historical fiction stories about England or the Navajo. Write about what happened when your grandparents were young. Interview your mother or father or some other adult. They're *all* older than you are! Imagine the history they must know! Interview them.

MYSTERY

Mystery stories are a game between the author and the reader. The author knows all the secrets and keeps the reader wondering—sometimes right up to the last line—how the mystery will be solved. In fantasy stories, the characters usually play the tricks. In mystery stories, the author gets to play the tricks.

Readers love to puzzle over puzzles, figure out riddles, and guess the answers to the mystery before the author is ready to reveal them. Who, or what, did it? The more mysterious the story, the better. The more danger our main character faces, the more we like it.

Authors tease us with hints and clues. A valuable painting is stolen. Someone is kidnapped. Dogs bark for no reason. Footsteps echo down empty halls. Something very mysterious is going on. But which clues will eventually lead us to the right answer? In a mystery story, two and two don't always add up to four.

Example

Mystery of the Disappearing Dogs by Barbara Brenner

Elena and Michael Garcia love their dog Perro. An old man whispers a warning to keep Perro on a leash. Perro gets away, and—*poof!*—he disappears. The mystery begins. The hardworking twins keep track of the facts in the case:

1. The old man warned them to keep Perro on a leash.
2. Perro was last seen chasing a peach-colored poodle being chased by a young woman with peach-colored hair.
3. A man in an apartment house says that dogs are disappearing in the neighborhood.
4. A woman at the animal shelter tells them about a ring of dognappers operating in the area.

As the story unfolds, the twins follow the clues. Things turn nasty. The dognappers kidnap Elena. Now her life is in danger. Michael thinks fast. By thinking about their clues and making some smart decisions, the twins escape injury and solve the mystery. In the end, the good guys win, the bad ones lose, and the dogs come home.

Three Important Things About a Mystery

1. Keep your story moving quickly so readers don't get bored.
2. Plant clues for your character to think about. Who else might

have done this? Did they have reasons? Could they have done it?

3. It is all right for some clues to throw your character off the trail as long as other clues are real and lead to the right answer. You can be tricky, but you can't be dishonest!

Four Rules for Mystery Stories

1. The character seems real.

2. The situation **prepares us for mystery**.

3. The problem seems believable **but unsolvable and maybe dangerous**.

4. The character **surprises us with a last-minute solution**.

TRY THIS

Practice Starting a Mystery Story

1. Start a page in your journal called MYSTERY.
2. Decide on a character for a mystery.
3. Create a mysterious situation that will involve your character.
4. Present your character with a tough, dangerous problem to solve.

Now you have the rules of five genres of stories, and you know what makes each kind different. If you have favorites, you know how to write them. But before your masterpiece is finished, you need two more things: Chapter Five and Chapter Six.

CHAPTER FIVE

Revising the First Draft

This chapter begins with a secret about revising. It's one of the most important secrets in the book. There are also four other reasons why this chapter is helpful:

✹ It shows you the difference between revising (this chapter) and rewriting (next chapter).

✹ You'll learn seven places to look for problems.

✹ There are tips for making your story stronger.

✹ You'll learn why reading your work aloud can be helpful.

Sooner or later you reach the end of your story. After all that hard work it feels good to write the last sentence! Most people quit right there. But that's why they're not writers. Here's the important secret that they don't know:

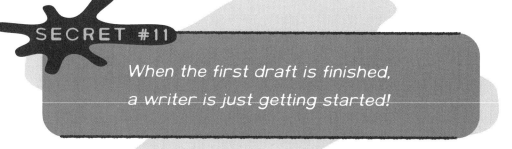

SECRET #11

When the first draft is finished, a writer is just getting started!

The best thing to do now is set your story aside for a while. Put it away and do something else. Read a book. Write in your journal. Start another story. Go shoot some hoops. The goal is to take your mind off the story you've been working on.

Why? Because when we are writing a story, we become part of our characters and their problems. It's like standing too close to a mirror. Our vision blurs, and it's hard to see the whole picture. Putting our story down for a while helps us stand back where we can see it all more clearly.

After a while we are ready to revise. The act of revising begins by asking ourselves questions. We ask questions about every element of our story, but they are all part of one main question. What we want to know is this:

DID I DO WHAT I SET OUT TO DO?

We must be very honest with ourselves when we answer this question. The truth, almost always, is no.

SECRET #12

Writers revise!

SECRET #13

The secret to good writing is good revising.

Revising is not the same thing as rewriting, which comes later. Revising gets at the "structure" of the story. It's about how we've put the parts together. Have I left out something that weakens the first draft? Have I put in too much and caused the story to swell up with unnecessary information? Does the action move swiftly? Does the solution make sense? *Did I do what I set out to do?*

This is the *first draft*. The story isn't finished yet. It isn't supposed to be perfect. Revising is part of writing. We expect to make changes at this stage — a lot of them!

Have you read Ann McGovern's picture book *Stone Soup*? A hungry young man promises a little old lady he can make soup by putting a stone into a pot of boiling water. Each time he samples the soup he says that it's good but would be better if the little old lady added something to help improve its taste. First she adds onions, then carrots, then a couple of plump chickens. After that she puts in some beef bones, a bit of pepper, a handful of salt, butter, and barley. And sure enough, that soup made from a stone tastes better and better!

The first draft of a story—yours or mine—is a pot of weak stone soup. It won't get better until we figure out what it needs. We make it stronger by adding and mixing the right ingredients: a pinch more of this, a dash of that. When we're done, our readers will enjoy a tastier story.

Reading our story aloud helps. We hear how our words go together, and our ears tell us where we may have a problem to work on. Ask family members or friends to listen to you read your story and give you their observations. If reading to family and friends doesn't work out, don't give up! Stand up and read your story to yourself.

My favorite place to read aloud is in our living room, facing a window onto the backyard. Sometimes my only audience is sparrows chattering among themselves in the hackberry trees.

After you read your story aloud and gather observations, what's next? Take up your pencil like a sword and march on the hobgoblins gnawing at the timbers of your first draft. Ruthlessly roust them out! Mark all over that wonderful, perfect draft! Chances are the draft is not wonderful. Not yet. And I promise you it is still far from perfect.

When I finish whacking my way through a first draft, you ought to see all the circles and underlines and crossed-out sections and question marks and lines with arrows showing where I should move this sentence or insert a new paragraph! It looks like what it is: a battleground. But I won, and winning makes me happy because I'm that much closer to finishing my story. After you've revised a few times, you'll recognize hobgoblins on sight. Until then, here is a list of places to look for them:

SEVEN PLACES TO LOOK

1. Beginning

2. Characters

3. Situation

4. Problem

5. Action

6. Solution

7. Ending

SECRET #14

*When we revise, we improve on **how** we tell our story.*

Revising isn't hard if we take it in steps. From the list above, we'll tackle one part at a time. Let's start with the beginning. I'll show you what to look for. When we revise, we have to think like two people at once: the writer and the reader.

Beginning

Don't forget: If we don't catch that reader in the beginning, we won't get another chance! Pick up one of your favorite books, read the first paragraph, then try to stop reading and put it down. Hard to do, isn't it? That's because the author did a good job of capturing your interest.

That's what you want to do with the beginning of your story, too. Here's a checklist that helps us ask the right questions:

- Does it get off to a fast start?
- How well does it catch the reader's interest?
- Do we meet the main character right away?
- How quickly do we set up the situation for the story?
- How soon do we discover the character's problem—or at least get a hint about what it might be?

As you review each point on the list, make notes about what you think. See why first drafts get marked up? Problems practically leap off the page, screaming, "I need help! I need more 'gotcha'!"

Now you're getting into the spirit of revising. Go over your notes and use them to make your beginning stronger.

Characters

Strong characters help make strong stories. When we finish reading a story, we remember our favorite characters. We remember the villains, too, but we root for the "good guys" to win.

What do we want from our characters? Here's a checklist:

- Do we like our main character?
- What are the traits that make us like him or her?
- Does the main character also have a few faults?
- Are they the kind of faults that we can forgive, like being forgetful, impatient, or klutzy?
- Do we want the main character to succeed?

In Chapter Two, you made a list of favorite characters. Thinking about strong characters in other writers' stories helps us think of ways to improve the ones in our own stories. You may notice that good characters are not always perfect. A hero who is perfect all the time could be pretty hard to take. Remember that Kara lied to her classmates even though, in the end, she told the truth and apologized.

And bad characters may not always be rotten through and through. Kara's classmates taunted her into making a mistake but, by the end of the story, they listened to her and asked questions about her life on the ranch.

Now check your notes and look for ways to make your characters stronger.

Situation

The three most important elements of a story are character, situation, and problem. When we thought about changing Kara's situation, her character and her problem had to change, too, to make sense in the new situation. The situation makes the story seem possible and believable, even if the story is a fairy tale.

As you read over your first draft, ask yourself if you have created a situation that makes your story seem possible and believable. Here's a checklist:

- **Am I telling my readers what they need to know to understand how my story could happen?**
- **Am I using enough "senses" descriptions to help the reader "be there"?**
- **Does my character seem to belong in this situation?**
- **Do the problems he or she faces make sense?**

Be critical. The reader will be. Make honest notes, and then use them to make your situation work better for your story.

Problem

Every story presents the main character with at least one problem. Problems come in all sizes and shapes. A girl lies to her classmates and has to figure out what to do about it. A puppy gets lost and has to find his way back home. An old man wants to give his wife a birthday gift, but he has no money.

The problem must be big enough and serious enough to capture your readers' imagination and keep them reading. When you read the problem in your story, don't forget to read it as a writer and also as a reader. Here are some questions you might ask:

- **Does my character's problem seem real?**
- **Is it important? (What would happen if the problem doesn't get solved?)**
- **Is it the kind of problem that makes me want to find out how the character can solve it?**

Think about your character's problem while you make your notes. If you think the problem could use a little work, get out that pencil.

Action

This is the main part of your story. It's where your character tries, and fails, and tries again, and fails again, and keeps on trying until he or she finally solves the problem or learns to cope with it. The action in a lot of stories could be outlined like this:

- The first idea seems sure to work.
- But it fails!
- Now things look even worse.
- Our character thinks of an even better idea.

- ☀ But something else goes wrong instead!
- ☀ Things seem impossible.
- ☀ The character is doomed!
- ☀ Until finally—at the last possible second, against all odds—the third idea, which is smarter and more dangerous and braver than all the others, works!

This is the longest part of your story, and it will probably take the longest time to revise. As you reread your first draft, take a careful look at how your character attempts to solve his or her problem. Here's a checklist:

- ☀ **How many times does my main character try to solve the problem?**
- ☀ **Does each attempt seem logical at the time?**
- ☀ **Each time my character fails, does it seem to make matters even worse?**
- ☀ **Does my character learn something from his or her failures that leads to the final solution?**

After you make your notes you may find yourself writing again. Maybe your character hasn't tried hard enough, or often enough, to solve the problem. Maybe he or she hasn't planned enough or talked enough to show us what might happen next. Remember, readers like to see the hero sweat. Maybe you need to make your main character wait a little longer before tasting sweet victory!

Solution

In Chapter Two, I told you that the solution usually comes when the character finally understands that there is only one way to get the job done. The solution may be risky, hard, even dangerous, but it's the only way. When we understand what he or she is about to do, and why it is so necessary, we follow along, rooting silently for the hero to make it.

How does the main character in your story decide on the final answer to his or her problem? This is a crucial point in any story. After all the confusion and failure, the end is near. The solution is coming toward us, fast.

To make sure that your solution seems logical and exciting and believable, ask yourself these questions:

- **Does my main character finally understand what he or she must do to solve the problem?**
- **Does my character show us through action and dialogue what he or she is about to attempt?**
- **Is there some risk involved?**
- **If the character fails, what will happen?**
- **Is the solution, when it comes, exciting?**
- **Is it believable?**

Ending

In Chapter Three, we talked about how the beginning and the ending go together. We begin with the ending in mind. We end with the beginning in mind. That's because readers—like all people—remember how something ends, whether it's a favorite song, a movie, or your story.

Remember that the solution is not quite the same thing as the ending. At least it doesn't have to be. The solution comes when the main character solves the problem. In the ending, we wrap up the whole story in a way that leaves the reader nodding his or her head in satisfaction. It's our chance to tie up loose ends. And, often, we find a way to remind the reader of how far we've come from the beginning of the story.

Read the beginning and ending of your first draft and ask yourself these questions:

- **Do they seem to belong to the same story?**
- **If the beginning gave a clue about where the story might lead, does the ending seem logical?**
- **Does anything about the ending remind us of something at the beginning?**

If you don't feel good about the way the first draft ends, your reader probably won't, either. So change it now. Revise it. You will be glad you did.

Finished? Make a clean copy of the revised draft. Get used to making clean copies. Since writers revise many times, they spend a lot of time making new copies. Now you can read your revised draft with all those improvements and see for yourself how much better you've made it.

But don't think you're finished! In the next chapter you are going to mark all over your clean copy of the revised draft. Stop groaning. You want to be a writer? Okay, then. Turn the page. Bring your pencil.

We're headed toward the *finished story*!

CHAPTER SIX

Rewriting

In Chapter Five, we worked on revising. Now it's time to tackle the final process in writing a good story: rewriting.

✽ We'll begin with a list of places to troubleshoot.

✽ We'll work on four main areas and go over pointers on what to look for and how to improve your story.

✽ I'll give you six important ways to polish your writing.

Rewriting is different from revising. Revising is about structure and how we put the story together. Rewriting is about language and the way we tell the story. Rewriting gives us a chance to think about what we've said, and say it better.

SECRET #15

Writers rewrite.

Here's one way to do it:

1. Sit down with a clean copy of your revised draft.
2. Get out your pencil.
3. Read every word of the story.
4. Mark every spot that needs more work.

But I don't recommend going about it this way. Too loosey-goosey. No organization to it. It's better to start with a list of what you're looking for.

FOUR IMPORTANT THINGS TO LOOK FOR

1. Beginning
2. Language
3. Transition
4. Dialogue

Beginning

In the last chapter, we revised the beginning to get our story off to a good start. We made sure that we introduced our character, setting, and problem as quickly as possible. That's structure stuff, so it falls under revising. In this chapter we're rewriting, so we ask different questions.

The first thing we look at is language. Have we chosen strong nouns? Vigorous verbs? Imaginative expressions and comparisons? Or have we settled for soft-tire language with the air seeping out?

We get one chance to snatch the reader's attention. Let's not blow it with wimpy language. No matter how good the rest of the story is, we've got to entice the reader past the welcome mat at the front door.

SECRET #16

Writers work hard polishing beginnings.

Here are six **kinds of polish.**

1. Look for the best nouns and strongest verbs.
2. Don't let unnecessary adverbs slow you down.
3. Don't *tell* what's happening. *Show* it.
4. Work in the five senses to help the reader "be there."
5. Dialogue saves words and shows action.
6. Cut unnecessary words.

Example

Early one morning in 1811, the worst earthquake in our young nation's history struck Missouri. Here is one way a story about it might begin for a pioneer family living in a cabin.

```
     Peter's bed was moving across the floor.
Ma was yelling loudly for him to wake up.
Dishes were flying quickly through the air.
The fireplace was falling apart, and the baby
was crying. Pa was carrying the baby and
pushing Ma and Peter out through the door.
They were having an earthquake!
```

In fifty-two words we meet Peter and his family, who live in a cabin and experience an earthquake. Not bad. We learn something about the characters, the setting, and the problem. But does the language sparkle? Nope. Get out the polish!

I've underlined what I think are a few problems: eight weak, boring verb forms and two unnecessary adverbs. Look at the paragraph again.

```
     Peter's bed was moving across the floor.
Ma was yelling loudly for him to wake up.
Dishes were flying quickly through the air.
The fireplace was falling apart, and the baby
was crying. Pa was carrying the baby and
pushing Ma and Peter out through the door.
They were having an earthquake!
```

Make the easy changes first. When we cut out two adverbs and replace passive verb forms with stronger active versions, we get this:

> Peter's bed <u>moved</u> across the floor. Ma <u>yelled</u> for him to wake up. Dishes <u>flew</u> through the air. The fireplace <u>fell</u> apart and the baby <u>cried</u>. Pa <u>carried</u> the baby and <u>pushed</u> Ma and Peter out through the door. They were having an earthquake!

Those simple changes put more zip in the opening. But all those ho-hum verbs need attention. There's nothing wrong with *moved*, *yelled*, *flew*, *fell*, *cried*, *carried*, and *pushed*. They just don't show much kick. What about adding some "sense words"? Maybe a little dialogue?

Similes make prose more interesting. You may already be

using similes in your writing but, in case you're not, here's a quick lesson. A simile is a comparison between two things, usually using "like" or "as."

- As light as air the butterfly touched her cheek.
- The garden hose reared up like a green cobra.
- She screamed as loud as a police siren.
- Dishes bounced off walls like startled quail.

> "Peter! Wake up!"
>
> Peter's bed bucked across the cabin floor. Dishes bounced off walls like startled quail. Fireplace stones cracked and thundered down in billows of ashy smoke.
>
> Clutching the screaming baby, Pa shoved Ma and Peter out the twisted doorway.
>
> "Earthquake!" he yelled. "Run for it!"

The original paragraph totaled fifty-two words. This rewritten version weighs in at forty-seven. We've found stronger verbs, introduced three senses (touch, smell, hearing), added dialogue and one simile, and saved five words.

Now look at your own beginning. See any rough spots? You now know where to polish.

TRY THIS

Practice Improving Your Beginning

1. Circle weak verb forms and unnecessary adverbs.
2. Make the easy changes first.
3. Introduce some of the five senses.
4. Use dialogue to help show action.
5. Look for places to use similes.
6. Cut unnecessary words.

Language

When you finish rewriting the opening of your revised draft, keep going. Everything we just talked about to make the beginning better makes the rest of the story better, too.

We writers collect words in our journals. We have favorite word-sounds. We search out new ways to say old things, admire brilliant phrases, catchy expressions, and clever similes. Loving language gives us patience to stay in the word-hunt until we bag those trophies we knew all along were there: the very way to say what we want to say.

SECRET #17

Writers adore language.

Transition

Stories are not all action all the time. Readers need a break now and then to catch their breath and get ready for what comes next. *Transition* takes us from one action scene to the next. Whether we're changing time, location, or characters, transition passages get the job done.

Example

"The Giant Who Threw Tantrums" from *The Book of Giant Stories* by David L. Harrison

Beginning

```
    At  the  foot  of  Thistle  Mountain  lay  a
village.

    In the village lived a little boy who liked
to go walking.

    One Saturday afternoon he was walking in the
woods when he was startled by a terrible noise.

    He scrambled behind a bush.

    Before  long  a  huge  giant  came  stamping
down the path.

    He looked upset.
```

Action

"Tanglebangled ringlepox!" the giant bellowed. He banged his head against a tree until the leaves shook off like snowflakes.

"Franglewhangled whippersnack!" the giant roared.

Yanking up the tree, he whirled it around his head and knocked down twenty-seven other trees.

Muttering to himself, he stalked up the path toward the top of Thistle Mountain.

Transition

The little boy hurried home.

Action

"I just saw a giant throwing a tantrum!" he told everyone in the village.

They only smiled.

"There's no such thing as a giant," the mayor assured him.

"He knocked down twenty-seven trees," said the little boy.

"Must have been a tornado," the weatherman said with a nod. "Happens around here all the time."

Transition

> The next Saturday afternoon the little boy
> again went walking. Before long he heard a
> horrible noise. Quick as lightning, he
> slipped behind a tree.

Go through your manuscript and circle the transitions that take your story from one action scene to the next. I bet you have some even if you didn't know what they were when you wrote them.

Make sure that each transition does its job with as few words as possible. Cut out anything that doesn't move your story along. These passages may be quiet, but they play a mighty role in your story's success. Treat them well.

SECRET #18

Writers love words but use as few as possible.

DIALOGUE

Dialogue covers a lot of action in a hurry. When we played with the fox sneaking up on the henhouse full of kickboxing chickens, the scene grew more interesting with dialogue.

> Unaware that he was being watched, Fox
> crept up the path.
>
> "Ready, girls?" Lily whispered.

> "Let him come!" came two dozen fierce
> voices.

Dialogue saves unnecessary words, helps the reader understand our characters, and shows action instead of telling about it. In the second version of the boy with a mouse, we used this line:

> "I'll find her," he assures himself. "Last
> time, she was in the bathroom."

That's thirteen words. Say the same thing without dialogue, and you get something like this:

> He felt sure that he would find her. The
> last time, she was in the bathroom.

That's three words longer and half as interesting. This is a serious moment in the boy's story, a turning point. His pet is missing. At a time like this we don't want the author to tell us what the boy is thinking. We want the boy to show us.

TRY THIS

Practice Changing Narration to Dialogue

1. Look for places in your story where you can let one or more of your characters speak.
2. See if your story moves faster when characters tell us how they feel and what they think.
3. Instead of describing your main character, use dialogue to let one of your other characters do it.

GRAMMAR, PUNCTUATION, AND SPELLING

Notice what comes last? Last doesn't mean least. Last means that after everything else is done, we have one more job to do. After company leaves, we tidy up the house. It wouldn't make sense to do it while we're entertaining and making the mess.

For the same reason, writers don't stop to look up every word and fret over commas when we're still revising and rewriting. But when everything else is done, we get busy making our manuscript as correct as possible.

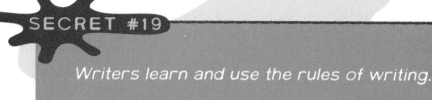

SECRET #19

Writers learn and use the rules of writing.

This is the time we look for misspelled words, check punctuation, and correct grammar. If you're not sure, look it up. It's fair to ask for help from someone who knows. This next clean copy you make is the last one. It's the *final manuscript*!

I love it that you want to write. I can't think of anything more pleasant to wish you than to become a writer. In the Introduction (which you may have skipped over), I gave you the first two secrets in this book. In case you missed them, here they are again.

SECRET #20

The better a writer does his or her job, the easier it looks.

SECRET #21

If you follow a few guidelines, you can turn your story into a winner.

Now you understand these writing secrets and many others that you have discovered on your own. The first six chapters have provided tips about writing and plenty of practice.

You have come a long way. You are becoming a writer. And, as a writer, you understand how important reading is to a writer. The relationship between reading and writing is so important that the last chapter is about that connection.

CHAPTER SEVEN

Becoming a Writer

This final chapter is short but important. It is here to remind you that we writers are dedicated to what we do. Writing is fun and it's also work. I'll break this chapter into four sections:

* Writers read.

* Writers write.

* Writers make time to do what they have to do.

* And, for those who still think they are too busy to write, seven ways to create more writing time.

Writers are readers. We read for the same reason that anyone else does: for the pleasure of sitting down with a friendly book. But then we take reading one step further. We also read to study good writing and see how others do it. You can't become a writer if you don't become a reader.

SECRET #22

Not all readers write, but all writers read.

What if your teacher told you that you could become a writer? Would you do it? I bet you would. After all, you are reading this book, and you are already writing.

What if your teacher told every student in the room that he or she could become a writer? Would they all become writers? Probably not.

There is a reason for that. Becoming a writer is a decision we have to make on our own. It helps a lot to have someone encourage us, but we're the only ones who can make the final decision. Only we can make the commitment.

SECRET #23

*The first step to becoming a writer
is making the commitment to become a writer.*

Writers are committed to writing. You don't have to go around jabbing a pencil in the air or talking about writing to everyone you meet. You don't have to buy yourself a writer's outfit. But you do need to practice your commitment to writing. People say this to writers all the time: "Someday, when I have more time, I'm going to start writing."

I hope they do. But probably they will never become writers. Why?

SECRET #24

Only those who write become writers.

That's pretty simple. But truth is simple. Musicians practice regularly. Athletes work out on a schedule. Successful people set routines and stick to them. Writers create time to write. You have to figure out the best time and place to do your work. Then get busy.

SECRET #25

Writers don't make excuses. They make time.

It is amazing how much you can write, a little at a time.
The main thing is to be consistent. Nobody starts and finishes a story in one sitting. We create our stories one word at a time, like masons building brick by brick.

If you write ten minutes a day, six days a week, that's an hour of writing. In forty weeks, you'll write for forty hours, the same as a week of eight-hour days.

Maybe you can't write at the same time every day. There will be days when you can't squeeze in another thing. The trick is to look for times that do work. I know this from experience: If you make a writing schedule that works for you, you're far more likely to stick to it.

SEVEN WAYS TO WORK IN SOME WRITING

1. Carry a small notebook and pen.

2. If you do your best thinking in the tub or shower, keep a pad and pencil close by.

3. Between your house and school you may come up with the perfect word or expression for that story you're working on.

4. Go to bed fifteen minutes earlier and get up fifteen minutes earlier in the morning to write.

5. Work in some writing on trips and vacations.

6. Write more during summers and holidays.

7. Trade off a little time on the phone, computer, and television to write.

Remember SECRETS NUMBER TWENTY-FOUR AND TWENTY-FIVE:

Only those who write become writers!

Writers don't make excuses. They make time.

Here is where we part company. I hope you keep writing. I'll think of you, jotting in your journal, or curled up with a book, or maybe watching people go by and making up stories about them. I'll be doing those things, too.

While I was growing up, my passions were art, reading, music, baseball, nature, and science. When a teacher in college said I could write, I wasn't sure what he meant, exactly. But by the time I sold my first book—eight years and 152 submissions later—I knew. Writers are people who don't give up. Writing becomes who we are. It is our way of being.

Writing makes me happy. Unless I'm traveling, I work at home in my office forty hours each week. First drafts are in pencil. When I revise and rewrite, the computer creates fresh copies of the ten-to-twenty successive versions. How do I feel, being a writer? Fantastic! I'm proud to be among those authors who take their responsibility seriously and work hard to write good books for young people. Some of the best writers in the world write for kids.

After publishing seven books of poetry, twenty books of nonfiction, and thirty-four books of fiction, I wanted to share what I've learned so far. Writing this book made me feel closer than ever to you, the reader. Writers and readers meet and become friends on the pages of a book. This time you're the reader. One day, before long I hope, you'll be the writer.

BOOKS BY DAVID L. HARRISON

Poetry
The Mouse Was Out at Recess, Boyds Mills Press, 2003
The Alligator in the Closet, Boyds Mills Press, 2003
Wild Country, Boyds Mills Press, 1999
The Purchase of Small Secrets, Boyds Mills Press, 1998
The Boy Who Counted Stars, Boyds Mills Press, 1994
A Thousand Cousins, Boyds Mills Press, 1996
Somebody Catch My Homework, Boyds Mills Press, 1993

Fiction
Dylan the Eagle-Hearted Chicken, Boyds Mills Press, 2002
The Book of Giant Stories, Boyds Mills Press, 2001
Johnny Appleseed: My Story, Random House, 2001
Farmer's Garden, Boyds Mills Press, 2000
The Animals' Song, Boyds Mills Press, 1997
When Cows Come Home, Boyds Mills Press, 1994
Wake Up, Sun!, Random House, 1986

Nonfiction
Writing Stories (Scholastic Guides), Scholastic, 2004
Oceans: The Vast, Mysterious Deep, Boyds Mills Press, 2003
Volcanoes: Nature's Incredible Fireworks, Boyds Mills Press, 2002
Rivers: Nature's Wondrous Waterways, Boyds Mills Press, 2002
Caves: Mysteries Beneath Our Feet, Boyds Mills Press, 2001

For Teachers
*Using the Power of Poetry to Teach Language Arts, Social Studies,
    Math, and More*, With Kathy Holderith, Scholastic, 2003
Easy Poetry Lessons That Dazzle and Delight, With Bernice E.
    Cullinan, Scholastic, 1999